THEATER OF THE OPPRESSED

17

Theater of the Oppressed

Augusto Boal

Translated from Spanish by Charles A. and
Maria-Odilia Leal McBride and Emily Fryer

Pluto  Press
LONDON

First published in 1979 by Pluto Press
345 Archway Road, London N6 5AA

New edition published 2000
Originally published in 1974 as
Teatro del Oprimido

British Library Cataloguing in Publication Data
A catalogue record for this book is available from
the British Library.

ISBN 0 7453 1658 1 hbk
ISBN 0 7453 1657 3 pbk

10 09 08 07 06 05 04 03 02 01

10 9 8 7 6 5 4 3 2

Printed in the European Union by
TJ International, Padstow, England

For
Fabián, Julián and Cecilia

Contents

Foreword

This book attempts to show that all theater is necessarily political, because all the activities of man are political and theater is one of them.

Those who try to separate theater from politics try to lead us into error — and this is a political attitude.

In this book I also offer some proof that the theater is a weapon. A very efficient weapon. For this reason one must fight for it. For this reason the ruling classes strive to take permanent hold of the theater and utilize it as a tool for domination. In so doing, they change the very concept of what "theater" is. But the theater can also be a weapon for liberation. For that, it is necessary to create appropriate theatrical forms. Change is imperative.

This work tries to show some of the fundamental changes and how the people have responded to them. "Theater" was the people singing freely in the open air; the theatrical performance was created by and for the people. It was a celebration in which all could participate freely. Then came the aristocracy and established divisions: some persons will go to the stage and only they will be able to act; the rest will remain seated, receptive, passive — these will be the spectators, the masses, the people. And in order that the spectacle may efficiently reflect the dominant ideology, the aristocracy established another division: some actors will be protagonists (aristocrats) and the rest will be the chorus — symbolizing, in one way or another, the mass. Aristotle's coercive system of tragedy shows us the workings of this type of theater.

Later came the bourgeoisie and changed these protagonists: they ceased to be objects embodying moral values, superstructural, and became multidimensional subjects, exceptional individuals, equally separated from the people, as new aristocrats — this is the poetics of *virtù* of Machiavelli.

Bertolt Brecht reacts to this poetics by taking the character theorized by Hegel as absolute subject and converting him back into an object. But now he is an object of social forces, not of the values of the superstructures. Social being determines thought, and not vice versa.

What was lacking to complete the cycle was what is happening at present in Latin America — the destruction of the barriers created by the ruling classes. First, the barrier between actors and spectators is destroyed: all must act, all must be protagonists in the necessary transformations of society. This is the process I describe in "Experiments with the People's Theater in Peru." Then the barrier between protagonists and choruses is destroyed: all must be simultaneously chorus and protagonist — this is the "Joker" system. Thus we arrive at the *poetics of the oppressed*, the conquest of the means of theatrical production.

Augusto Boal

Buenos Aires
July, 1974

Preface
The Unruly Protagonist

There are few surviving documents on the origins of Greek theater. With little documentary evidence and only fragmentary accounts, we can only guess at its beginning: we are condemned to use our imagination.

In Ancient Greece — as everywhere — after their arduous teamwork was over, workers liked to celebrate the suspension of Order. For teamwork to be possible, discipline is indispensable. When building a house, the painters cannot paint the walls before they have been erected; the roof can only be put in place after the foundations have been laid, never the other way round.

Rules are necessary for building work. But not once the job is done. At the "topping-off" party, when the house is finished, the builders have a beer, dance and sing, and open up a bit; they relax, and soon the barriers between them break down. Censorship sleeps and the mouth speaks. Mission accomplished, so the rules can be broken.

During harvest-time, farm workers would labor under strict discipline, from dawn to dusk, for weeks and months on end. First the grape harvest, then the winemaking. When it was over, of course they would get drunk, sing, and dance in homage to Dionysus, god of happiness, god of binges. Alcohol was essential, not accidental: it was the touch-paper of freedom. The celebrations of Greek farm laborers after harvest were just as spontaneous as those of builders today when they finish a house. The songs and dances came from the soul. It was creative anarchy — which could also play havoc. Freedom needed to be kept within bounds. There had to be limits. But can freedom in handcuffs be truly free? The aristocracy thought it could. As work had previously been disciplined, now freedom must be supervised, as if a threat. In extreme cases it could destroy what had been built.

A necessary contradiction. When it was free, the body could invent the dance, which came from inside; free, the body could dance in space and time. The choreographer turned up and charted the movement, explained the gesture, defined the rhythm, and limited the space. The dramatic poet came and wrote his verses. No more freed thought or creative chaos. Premeditated Order had arrived. Dramatic poetry and choreography were great advances, but freedom was over and done with. Something more solemn was introduced into the bacchanalian outbursts — the Dithyramb. This chorus was the imprisoned shout, clamor with rhyme and rhythm, an authorized implosion, civilized savagery, joy, measured out by the clock. What had hitherto not been a play became one. Now everyone danced the same dance and sang the same religious song.

*

Thespis was a multi-faceted figure: poet, choreographer, actor, and drunkard. He wrote poems and, blending into the Chorus, sang himself. He sketched out movements and performed them in the dithyrambic procession, in harmony with the Chorus. A true artist, he was true to himself.

One day, Solon the lawmaker came to see his play. Solon the Great, who had just revoked the Code of Drakon, whose memory still frightens us with a pre-Biblical "tooth-for-tooth" and "eye-for-eye." Solon was far-sighted; he was the legislator who went on to draw up democratic laws. To give you some idea of the kind of man he was, it seems to me that, among other qualities, he had the most marvelous intuition: he ruled that all citizens would be pardoned from any outstanding debts. What rejoicing! Clean slates all round: no one owed anything to anyone. Wonderful! Everyone who owed money loved the idea, although those to whom money was owed weren't so impressed. Solon pardoned all debts from then on, but he did not abolish the unjust, large estates which would cause many people to incur new and larger debts. Solon did everything by halves: he didn't end prostitution, but he was the first public man to set up red-light districts for public women. In fact, a large part of Greece was turned into just such a district. Solon the all-powerful came to see the play. Solon in the audience:

Zeus help us! There were shivers of excitement. Would he enjoy it? Solon came in leaning on his ivory stick, for he was lame, and sat in the front row. Solon, head of government, had his own very special seat.

Dithyrambs were religious processions (taking place in the fields), but there was, as there is today, a royal box, a kind of judging platform in front of which the Chorus would perform for the authorities with still more religious fervor. The play began modestly. In the middle of the poem, Thespis couldn't contain himself. He felt strange, and shouted: "Hold me up, I feel faint, I'm going to have a fit!" No one held him up. Then he jumped out of the Chorus and answered them. In the midst of his fit he began to say whatever came into his head. He was raving like a bacchant. He spoke about the city, about politics, men and laws. What at first had seemed to be merely an undisciplined actor's ad lib, an irresponsible joke, turned into a structured speech, which made it dangerous.

Shock! Horror! A simple Chorus member had dared to answer back. And before the Head of State. It *could* be done! And yet nobody had thought of it before. They had all been dutifully speaking in chorus: no one had realized that freedom was possible. Furiously Thespis addressed the Chorus with all his might. The Chorus sang in verse; he responded in prose. While the Chorus sang the accepted morality — religion — Thespis proclaimed his own ideas, adorned with his own words chosen on the spur of the moment as he thought fit. And fine words they were. This was puzzling: just what was going on? In the Chorus, everyone sings and dances in chorus, as they should. How could a man, even a Thespis, jump out of the rigid choreographic pattern and answer back, throw down a challenging "No" to a compulsory "Yes"?

Solon sat in silence and tried to take no notice, as if it was nothing to do with him, as though he hadn't heard right, as if he was slightly deaf. But after the show he sought out the actors in the dressing room to congratulate them. The popular lawmaker must do his duty. Pausing, he asked Thespis: "Aren't you ashamed to lie like that, deliberately, in front of so many people? Such a lovely Chorus, truthful, tuneful, orderly. Then you have to start telling barefaced lies!"

Thespis protested that he hadn't been lying: he had told his truth. Without realizing it, Thespis had created the Protagonist, the Proto, the First, the one who stands alone, the one who rebels, thinks and acts for himself — without mimesis, without mimicry, without imitating anyone. Finding out who he was, opening up new paths, revealing the possible,

Thespis was becoming a person who hurled himself into the unknown. He makes mistakes, but takes the consequences — as you sow, so shall you reap. Thespis looked Solon straight in the eye and answered him unabashed: "No, I'm not ashamed, worthy Solon, because I did not lie. What you saw isn't a portrayal of reality, it's a game!" He used the word "game" in the sense of interpretation, as the French say *jeu* or the English "play." What he really meant was theater, fiction, possibility, image or even, perhaps, representation of the real.

"All the same, it's a dangerous thing to do," retorted Solon. "The people might not understand your little game, and they could be influenced. After a while, this game, this lie, could pollute our culture — and there's nothing good in that. There's good in what the Chorus sings, in what's been written down and read by us, before being sung by you people. These freethinking notions are extremely dangerous."

To scare Thespis, he gave an example of a terrible punishment: "Look what happened to Prometheus: a good guy, but he made a bad move. He gave mankind fire, and that's dangerous. Fire burns. Prometheus set a bad example. He showed them that what belonged to the gods can be used by mortals. He played with fire and he burned his fingers. Prometheus ended up chained to a rock, his liver pecked out by vultures. Why? Because it starts with fire. But where does it end? Men are greedy, they always want more."

He concluded with this threat: "And the same thing will happen to you. What you actually said doesn't matter. It doesn't matter which words you used. What matters is that you demonstrated that things *could* be said. You showed them it was possible to speak out. You showed the people that each can think with his own head, choose his own words. This just won't do: it sets a bad example. *I* know that they can, but it must not be generally known."

Before he left, he growled: "Don't do it again, do you hear? I don't like it, not one little bit!" And with this terse phrase, Solon almost nipped western theater in the bud. But Thespis was stubborn, he was obstinate. Even with his back against the wall, he still wanted to continue being Protagonist. After all, it's delightful to be Protagonist. He wanted to go on living as a Protagonist, even if the Chorus kept to the text, singing the same song in the same key. It's hard to go back to a supporting role when you've been a Protagonist. Nobody enjoys that.

The audience at this memorable first night — not counting the usual handful of moaners — loved the idea. They wanted more. Improvisation is life. Deadlock. Now what? Thespis didn't want to give the impression of lying, and he didn't want to lie by saying he was lying. It would be a lie to say that he lied — it wasn't true that he lied. He had told his truth, which was one of the possible truths. The Chorus anxiously asked: "What now? So what do we do?" Nobody knew. "Can we or can't we? Do we cut it or don't we? We like it, but the big boss over there didn't seem to like it much. He pulled a face." Where was the truth, and where the lie? Thespis's truth negated the truth of the Chorus, which in turn negated his freedom. If anyone was lying, it wasn't him! So, now what?

So that no one would be lying and they could all tell their truth, Thespis, a creative man, had another marvelous idea. He invented disguise: the Mask (this, which looks like me, is not me, it is another — it is the Character); and Costume (I don't dress like this, it's the Character that dresses like this). And he wore buskins, the high boots of tragedy (I'm short, but the Character is tall, huge). Once in costume, the Character was no longer Thespis: it was the Other. Actor and Character, previously one and the same, were now separated and made into two: Man and Mask. Thespis could continue to be himself, by being disguised in the Other, inside the costume, on top of the buskins and behind the mask.

Because it was unreal, the actor's art became known in Greece as the art of Hypokrites, that is, he who pretended to be what he was not. He pretended to be by being, because it is clear that he was: if not, he couldn't be. Even if it was just an appearance, this appearance was. There were now two in the actor's art: the Actor, hidden behind the Mask, and the Mask itself. And so the actor's art was called — Hypocrisy. By the by, it is proven here that Theater and Hypocrisy emerged from the same matrix on the same day. This division of the one into two, this dichotomy between Actor and Character, has since been one of the most captivating themes of Theater — and of psychology.

Thespis had his creative way, but was forced to concede one important point. In the next season, he returned to look for his private Maecenas, protector of the arts. Plays were just as expensive to put on then as they are today: someone has to pay the production costs. The Maecenas of today are variously called: Angels on Broadway; *Ministère de la culture* in France, and Tax Breaks in Brazil; they existed then as now; they are as old as the hills. Thespis's producer was a kind-hearted millionaire who told him at once: "I quite understand, my dear Thespis. You are a true artist, a creator, a genius. I'm sure you will make history. The idea of inventing the Protagonist, who says whatever he wants, whatever comes into his head, is marvelous. Hearty congratulations!" Thespis was happy, but Maecenas hadn't finished. The worst was yet to come.

"The thing is, I'm not an actor, I'm a producer. Our names are linked. Whatever you say on stage, it's as if I were saying it myself. Look here, my dear Thespis, I can't put my money into a play if I'm only going to know the contents on the first night. I'm not being censorious, far from it. Every artist must be free. But before I spend my money, I need to know what I'm spending it on. It's right that you should say what you like, and it's right that I should only pay for what I like. In other words, if you want to keep getting my money, bring me the written script before you start rehearsals, because I don't like nasty surprises, do you hear? I don't just want to read the words of the Chorus, I want to read your Protagonist's improvisations as well!" Unfortunately, whenever improvisations are censored they stop being spur-of-the-moment creations. And Greek Theater, whatever historians may say, was subject to censorship. It was censored by Maecenas and those like him who, with their early tax incentives, would only pay for plays they approved of, and it was also censored by the priests of Dionysus. In the Acropolis in Athens you can still see the marble seat of the priest of Dionysus. There it stands, imposing and alone. The censor was right there in the front row.

*

Aeschylus, an aristocrat, invented the Deuteragonist. Now there were two protagonists, one able to agree with or contradict the other. Sophocles, another nobleman, invented the Tritagonist. Tragic poets now had three actors at their disposal, three hypocrites wearing masks. Each actor playing more than one part could increase the number of characters — he would not be recognized when he changed his Mask and altered his voice.

Hypocrisy was established once and for all. In this impossible divorce, the separation between Actor and Character, Thespis was both, as all good actors are. This was intricate Hypocrisy: the actor pretended to be what he was not and was what he pretended to be. It was all going too far: the Chorus continued to sing the Official History. But, with the invention of Dialogue, ideas were juxtaposed, and nothing guaranteed that the ideas supported by the authorities would prevail. Dialogue is always dangerous, because it creates discontinuity between one thought and another, between two opinions, or two possibilities — and between them infinity installs itself; so that all opinions are possible, all thoughts permitted. When Two have ceased to exist and only the Sole Absolute Thought remains, creation becomes impossible. Dialogue is Democracy.

The mere thought of this terrified Plato, who was so worried that he made a speech: "Now look here, all of you, I'm not having any of your theatrical nonsense in my Republic. It's unthinkable! It's not on! It's a damn pain! You can take your drama and stick it where the sun doesn't shine!" He went shouting through the streets, from door to door: "This world we live in is corrupt!" (He was quite right, too; he might have been talking about modern Brazil.) "It's the corruption of the ideal world, which is, yet does not exist, which is perfect, divine, marvelous, the World of Ideas. We are a pale reflection, a dim shadow of what we should be. The theater is even worse. It is the merest shadow of this shadow, most pallid pallidity, a sink of corruption. Down with Theater!"

Plato was furious: he was really angry. Aristotle wasn't; he shook his head, smiling, glad of the opportunity to contradict his master. "*Amicus Plato, sed magis amica Veritas!*" he said, in ancient Greek, which at the time was modern, but which has been handed down to us through Latin, a language in which Aristotle, it is safe to say, was far from fluent. In plain English, what Aristotle meant was that while he was Plato's friend (*Amicus Plato*), he was also a closer friend of Truth (*sed magis amica Veritas*).

Aristotle went on to explain: "Things are not exactly how Plato sees them. I don't think he has quite understood the question. In my view, the Protagonist can make all the mistakes he wants, even if the audience delights in his errors and shares his pleasures." He used the word *Empathia*, meaning that the audience so identified with the Protagonist that they momentarily interrupted their own thoughts and thought with the Protagonist's mind, that they dulled their emotions and felt his in place of theirs. In other words, it was the Prosthesis of Desire. The Protagonist, who had divorced himself from the actor, now married the overpowered Spectator, that is to say, he married the Prosthesis installed within the Spectator.

Aristotle continued: "But even if they are taking pleasure in something forbidden, it doesn't matter at all, because, as Thespis rightly said, it's a game, it's a representation." A man in the street, who was a disciple of

Plato, could not agree: "I think I get it, but all the same, if they find pleasure in the interpretation, they'll want to find pleasure, in reality. That's not on."

"That's just where you and Plato are completely wrong! Let them enjoy the mistake, sin as much as they like ... in fiction. All it needs is for things to go wrong for the Protagonist (and for the audience, who get pulled along with it) and there you have it. After a dazzling opening, everything falls apart in the middle of the Greek Tragedy. We'll call this reversal of fortune *Peripeteia* — it's best to give everything a name, it makes it all clearer, easier to understand. So the tragedy will have two parts, before and after the Peripeteia. First the pleasure, then the pain. And there should be a great big Catastrophe for the Protagonist at the end, if you'll permit me another technical term which I intend to use from now on."

"I see, the Protagonist gets a well-earned Catastrophe. But what about the audience? What do they get? What happens in the end?" asked the man in the street, puzzled. "They get Catharsis!," and he shouted: "You heard! Sock it to them, Catharsis! The audience are going to come out of the theater PURGED! The mistake — which if you don't mind I shall call Hamartia — the mistake is first aroused in the emotion of the audience, and is then expelled by reason."

"But the audience might switch off from the play when the reversal of fortune or, as you call it, Peripeteia begins. They might say: 'That would never happen to me.' Then they enjoy what they're going to enjoy and go away with a bad example in their minds, evil desires in their hearts, without appreciating the moral of the story."

Aristotle, whose ideas might have been on the conservative side, but who was clever nevertheless, explained his Machiavellian plan: "Listen, the audience is empathetically identified with the Protagonist. They think with his head, they feel with his heart. You only need the Protagonist to repent, to do a bit of *mea culpa*, and it'll be sorted. And I'm calling this confession Anagnorisis. Like it?" They all liked it and, even better, understood it.

Through Empathia — that precious and indispensable thing which marries Spectator and Protagonist, which prosthetically implants in the Spectator the desires of the Protagonist — the audience, hearing the hero's confession, will be making their own confession, promising themselves never to make mistakes again. The Protagonist's mistakes will do the job of sorting out the audience's behavior, of straightening out what's crooked. To quell any remaining doubts, he continued: "Listen, tragedy is the imitation of an action. But to imitate doesn't mean to copy, to ape something. It means to recreate the essence of what is created. It's a living, dynamic force. In this way the tragedy goes deep into the hearts of the audience and modifies any of their actions which are socially unacceptable."

Aristotle was so amazed by his own reasoning, so convinced by it, that he ran home to write a very clever book, to which he gave the delicious title *The Poetics* — a book which I recommend everyone to read closely. Year after year, century after century, this remained the Official History of Tragedy, and it was a fetter on the explosive Thespian tradition.

In the interest of truth, I must add two things. First, obviously not all Greek Tragedians, nor did they always, follow *The Poetics*. Some rebelled against it; many died before it was written; others weren't even aware of its contents. On the other hand, it existed as a model, something to aim for. Second, Aristotle wasn't as plainspoken as I have made him out to be. He was well educated, used to reading between the lines and spotting nuances. As for poor old me, I come from Penha, a working-class area in the north of Rio de Janeiro, where we call a spade a spade. So I have to be more direct, more objective. I have to tell the brutal truth! It's my destiny; I'm condemned to speak clearly.

*

Centuries later Brecht, writing about Aristotle, made a suggestion. He began by saying that this Empathia thing was all right for the ruling classes, who even ruled their characters' ideology; but it wouldn't suit the workers, for it helped perpetuate exploitation. So: down with Empathia. Instead, up with *Verfremdungseffekt*!

And what is this thing, this exotic term? *Verfremdungseffekt* means to watch from a distance, without involving oneself, as one who observes, thinks and draws his or her own conclusions. The actor is no longer hidden behind the Mask; he emerges and reveals himself beside it, openly contradicts it, and enters into conflict with it. What Thespis had done with the Chorus, Brecht now did with the Protagonist through the *Verfrendungs*. The duality, which formerly had been cemented in the challenge between Protagonist and Chorus, now became a challenge between Actor and Character. The real Unruly Protagonist was now the Actor (and the Poet), not the Character!

In Brecht's plays, however, the unbridgeable gulf between stage and audience remains. The stage belongs to the characters and the actors. Even when the dramatist is critical of what the Character does, when he denounces him, it is the Dramatist or the Actor who criticizes, not the audience. By way of songs, narration, and distancing, the dramatist reveals things and in so doing reveals himself. He exposes his thoughts. He doesn't hide behind his characters; he doesn't merge with them. But the stage remains his private property, his space, his territory.

The spectator, who sits stock-still, is encouraged to think in a way which is presented as being the right way of thinking, the Truth. It is the dramatist who tells this Truth, who points the way: he is affirming, not asking. We are a long way from Socratic dialogue and close to the Democratic Centralism of some political parties.

As we know, to speak is to take power: whenever we become the speaker we are empowered. Even in Brecht, it is the dramatist, not the citizen, who chooses the word. It is true that at one time Brecht tried more participative forms of theater. He foresaw the future mobilization of the audience. In some of his poems he foresaw the possible use of the theater by audiences turned actors. But in his great dramas, the wall between stage and audience did not come down. As for me, I am *amicus Verfremdungseffekt*. But one can go further, I think. *Sed magis amica Theatrum Opressi.*

It is an enormous advance not to let oneself be invaded by the characters. We don't allow ourselves to be invaded, but — is that all there is to it? Should actors and characters go on dominating the stage, their domain, while I sit still in the audience? I think not. I think we could go much further: we need to invade! The audience mustn't just liberate its Critical Conscience, but its body too. It needs to invade the stage and transform the images that are shown there.

To transform is to be transformed. The action of transforming is, in itself, transforming.

The members of the audience must become the Character: possess him, take his place — not obey him, but guide him, show him the path they think right. In this way the Spectator becoming Spect-Actor is democratically opposed to the other members of the audience, free to invade the scene and appropriate the power of the actor. With their hearts and minds the audience must rehearse battle plans — ways of freeing themselves from all oppressions.

The Unruly Protagonist separated himself from the Chorus. He rebelled. The Mask hid the Actor behind the Character. Realistic theater melded the two together again, dissolving the Actor, who was subjected to the empathetic command of the Character. Brecht proposed to separate Actor and Character once again, so that the Spectator could contemplate them both at the same time and wonder: me or him? But Brecht eventually accepted the marriage of the Poet (through the Actor) and the Spectator, who continued to supervise, in the same way as husbands once did to wives in old-fashioned marriages. The Poet wears the trousers and says what goes. The Spectator is still cast as an old-fashioned wife.

*

I, Augusto Boal, want the Spectator to take on the role of Actor and invade the Character and the stage. I want him to occupy his own Space and offer solutions.

By taking possession of the stage, the Spect-Actor is consciously performing a responsible act. The stage is a representation of the reality, a fiction. But the Spect-Actor is not fictional. He exists in the scene and outside of it, in a dual reality. By taking possession of the stage in the fiction of the theater he acts: not just in the fiction, but also in his social reality. By transforming fiction, he is transformed into himself.

This invasion is a symbolic trespass. It symbolizes all the acts of trespass we have to commit in order to free ourselves from what oppresses us. If we do not trespass (not necessarily violently), if we do not go beyond our cultural norms, our state of oppression, the limits imposed upon us, even the law itself (which should be transformed) — if we do not trespass in this we can never be free.. To free ourselves is to trespass, and to transform. It is through a creation of the new that that which has not yet existed begins to exist. To free yourself is to trespass. To trespass is to exist. To free ourselves is to exist.

To free yourself is to exist.

Aristotle's
Coercive System
of Tragedy

[Athens] was governed in the name of the people, but in the spirit of the nobility. . . . The only "progress" consisted in the displacement of the aristocracy of birth by an aristocracy of money, of the clan state by a plutocratic rentier state. . . . She was an imperialistic democracy, carrying on a policy which gave benefits to the free citizens and the capitalists at the cost of the slaves and those sections of the people who had no share in the war profits.

*   *   *   *   *

Tragedy is the characteristic creation of Athenian democracy; in no form of art are the inner conflicts of its social structure so directly and clearly to be seen as in this. The externals of its presentation to the masses were democratic, but its content, the heroic sagas with their tragi-heroic outlook on life, was aristocratic. . . . It unquestionably propagates the standards of the great-hearted individual, the uncommon distinguished man . . . it owed its origin to the separation of the choir-leader from the choir, which turned collective performance of songs into dramatic dialogue. . . .

*   *   *   *   *

The tragedians are in fact state bursars and state purveyers — the state pays them for the plays that are performed, but naturally does not allow pieces to be performed that would run counter to its policy or the interests of the governing classes. The tragedies are frankly tendentious and do not pretend to be otherwise.

Arnold Hauser, *The Social History of Art*[1]

Introduction

The argument about the relations between theater and politics is as old as theater and . . . as politics. Since Aristotle, and in fact since long before, the same themes ,and arguments that are still brandished were already set forth. On one hand, art is affirmed to be pure contemplation, and on the other hand, it is considered to present always a vision of the world in transformation and therefore is inevitably political insofar as it shows the means of carrying out that transformation or of delaying it.

Should art educate, inform, organize, influence, incite to action, or should it simply be an object of pleasure? The comic poet Aristophanes thought that "the dramatist should not only offer pleasure but should, besides that, be a teacher of morality and a political adviser." Eratosthenes contradicted him, asserting that the "function of the poet is to charm the spirits of his listeners, never to instruct them." Strabo argued: "Poetry is the first lesson that the State must teach the child; poetry is superior to philosophy because the latter is addressed to a minority while the former is addressed to the masses." Plato, on the contrary, thought that the poets should be expelled from a perfect republic because "poetry only makes sense when it exalts the figures and deeds that should serve as examples; theater imitates the things of the world, but the world is no more than a mere imitation of ideas — thus theater comes to be an imitation of an imitation."

As we see, each one has his opinion. Is this possible? Is the

tion of art to the spectator something that can be diversely interpreted, or, on the contrary, does it rigorously obey certain laws that make art either a purely contemplative phenomenon or a deeply political one? Is one justified in accepting the poet's declared intentions as an accurate description of the course followed in his works?

Let us consider the case of Aristotle, for example, for whom poetry and politics are completely different disciplines, which must be studied separately because they each have their own laws and serve different purposes and aims. To arrive at these conclusions, Aristotle utilizes in his *Poetics* certain concepts that are scarcely explained in his other works. Words that we know in their current connotation change their meaning completely if they are understood through the *Nicomachaean Ethics* or the *Magna Moralia*.

Aristotle declares the independence of poetry (lyric, epic, and dramatic) in relation to politics. What I propose to do in this work is to show that, in spite of that, Aristotle constructs the first, extremely powerful poetic-political system for intimidation of the spectator, for elimination of the "bad" or illegal tendencies of the audience. This system is, to this day, fully utilized not only in conventional theater, but in the TV soap operas and in Western films as well: movies, theater, and television united, through a common basis in Aristotelian poetics, for repression of the people.

But, obviously, the Aristotelian theater is not the only form of theater.

Art Imitates Nature

The first difficulty that we face in order to understand correctly
the workings of tragedy according to Aristotle stems from the
very definition which that philosopher gives of art. What is art,
any art? For him, it is an imitation of nature. For us, the word
"imitate" means to make a more or less perfect copy of an original model. Art would, then, be a copy of nature. And "nature"
means the whole of created things. Art would, therefore, be a
copy of created things.

But this has nothing to do with Aristotle. For him, to imitate
(mimesis) has nothing to do with copying an exterior model.
"Mimesis" means rather a "re-creation." And nature is not the
whole of created things but rather the creative principle itself.
Thus when Aristotle says that art imitates nature, we must understand that this statement, which can be found in any modern
version of the *Poetics,* is due to a bad translation, which in turn
stems from an isolated interpretation of that text. "Art imitates
nature" actually means: "Art re-creates the creative principle of
created things."

In order to clarify a little more the process and the principle
of "re-creation" we must, even if briefly, recall some philosophers who developed their theories before Aristotle.

The School of Miletus.

Between the years 640 and 548 B.C., in the Greek city of

Miletus, lived a very religious oil merchant, who was also a navigator. He had an immovable faith in the gods; at the same time, he had to transport his merchandise by sea. Thus he spent a great deal of his time praying to the gods, begging them for good weather and a calm sea, and devoted the rest of his time to the study of the stars, the winds, the sea, and the relations between geometrical figures. Thales — this was the Greek's name — was the first scientist to predict an eclipse of the sun. A treatise on nautical astronomy is also attributed to him. As we see, Thales believed in the gods but did not fail to study the sciences. He came to the conclusion that the world of appearances — chaotic and many-sided though it was — actually was nothing more than the result of diverse transformations of a single substance, water. For him, water could change into all things, and all things could likewise be transformed into water. How did this transformation take place? Thales believed that things possessed a "soul." Sometimes the soul could become perceptible and its effects immediately visible: the magnet attracts the iron — this attraction is the "soul." Therefore, according to him, the soul of things consists in the movement inherent in things which transforms them into water and that, in turn, transforms the water into things.

Anaximander, who lived not long afterward (610-546 B.C.) held similar beliefs, but for him the fundamental substance was not water, but something indefinable, without predicate, called *apeiron*, which according to him, created things through either condensing or rarifying itself. The apeiron was, for him, divine, because it was immortal and indestructible.

Another of the philosophers of the Milesian school, Anaximenes, without varying to any great extent from the conceptions just described, affirmed that air was the element closest to immateriality, thus being the primal substance from which all things originated.

In these three philosophers a common trait can be noted: the search for a single substance whose transformations give birth to all known things. Furthermore, the three argue, each in his own way, for the existence of a transforming force, immanent to the substance — be it air, water, or apeiron. Or four elements, as Empedocles asserted (air, water, earth, and fire); or numbers, as Pythagoras believed. Of all of them, very few written texts have come down to us. Much more has remained of Heraclitus, the first dialectician.

Heraclitus and Cratylus.

For Heraclitus, the world and all things in it are in constant flux, and the permanent condition of change is the only unchangeable thing. The appearance of stability is a mere illusion of the senses and must be corrected by reason. And how does change take place? Well, all things change into fire, and fire into all things, in the same manner that gold is transformed into jewelry which can in turn be transformed into gold again. But of course gold does not transform itself; it is transformed. There is someone (the jeweler), foreign to the matter gold, who makes the transformation possible. For Heraclitus, however, the transforming element would exist within the thing itself, as an opposing force. "War is the mother of all things; opposition unifies, for that which is separated creates the most beautiful harmony; all that happens, only happens because there is struggle." That is to say, each thing carries within itself an antagonism which makes it move from what it is to what it is not.

To show the constantly changing nature of all things, Heraclitus used to offer a concrete example: nobody can step into the same river twice. Why? Because on the second attempt it will not be the same waters that are running, nor will it be exactly the same person who tries it, because he will be older, even if by only a few seconds.

His pupil, Cratylus, even more radical, would say to his teacher that nobody can go into a river even once, because upon going in, the waters of the river are already moving (which waters would he enter?) and the person who would attempt it would already be aging (who would be entering, the older or the younger one?). Only the movement of the waters is eternal, said Cratylus; only aging is eternal; only movement exists: all the rest is appearance.

Parmenides and Zeno.

On the extreme opposite of those two defenders of movement, of transformation, and of the inner conflict which promotes change, was Parmenides, who took as the point of departure for the creation of his philosophy a fundamentally logical premise: being is and non-being is not. Actually it would be absurd to think the opposite and, said Parmenides, absurd thoughts are not real. There is, therefore, an identity between being and thinking, according to the philosopher. If we accept this initial premise, we are obliged to derive from it a number of consequences:

1) Being is one (indivisible), for if it were not so, between one being and another there would be non-being, which in fact would divide them; but since we have already accepted that non-being is not, we have to accept that being is one, in spite of the deceptive appearance that tells us the opposite.

2) Being is eternal, for if it were not so, after being there would necessarily come non-being which, as we have seen, is not.

3) Being is infinite. (Here Parmenides made a small logical mistake: after affirming that being is infinite, he asserted that it was also spherical; now if it is spherical it has a shape, and therefore has a limit, beyond which there necessarily would come non-being. But these are subtleties which should not concern us here. Possibly "spherical" is a bad translation, and Parmenides might have meant "infinite," in all directions, or something like that.)

4) Being is unchangeable, because all transformation means that being stops being what it is in order to begin to be what it is not yet: between one state and the other there would necessarily be non-being, and since the latter is not, there is no possibility (according to this logic) of change.

5) Being is motionless: movement is an illusion, because motion means that being moves from the place where it is to the place where it is not, this meaning that between the two places there would be non-being, and once more this would be a logical impossibility.

From these statements, Parmenides ends by concluding that since they are in disagreement with our senses, with what we can see and hear, this means that there are two perfectly definable worlds: the intelligible, rational world, and the world of appearances. Motion, according to him, is an illusion, because we can demonstrate that it does not actually exist; the same for the multiplicity of existing things, which are in his logic, a single being, infinite, eternal, unchangeable.

Like Heraclitus, Parmenides too, had his radical disciple, named Zeno. The latter had the habit of telling two stories to prove the inexistence of motion. Two famous stories, which are worth remembering. The first said that in a race between Achilles (the greatest Greek runner) and a turtle, the former could never reach the latter if it were allowed a small lead at the start. Zeno's reasoning went like this: no matter how fast Achilles may run, he will first have to cover the distance that separated him from the turtle when the race started. But no matter how slow the turtle may be, it will have moved, even if only a few centimeters. When Achilles attempts to overtake it once again, he will, nonetheless, have to cover this second distance. During this time the turtle will have advanced somewhat more, and to overtake it, Achilles will have to cover the distance — smaller and smaller each time — that will be separating him from the turtle, which, very slowly, will never let itself be defeated.

The second story, or example, states that if an archer shoots an arrow toward someone, the latter will not have to get out of the way because the arrow will never reach him. The same is true if a rock falls from above one's head: he does not have to flee because the rock will never break his head. Why? Very simple, Zeno would say (obviously a man of the extreme right), because an arrow or a rock, in order to move, like any thing or person, must move either in the place where it is or in the place where it is not yet. It can not move in the place where it is, because if it is there this means it has not moved. Neither can it move in the place where it is not, because of course it will not be there to make the move. The story is told that when rocks were thrown at him for engaging in reasoning like this, Zeno, in spite of his logic, used to flee.

Zeno's logic clearly suffers from a fundamental fault: the movements of Achilles and the turtle are not interdependent or discontinuous: Achilles does not first gain one part of the distance to be run, in order then to run the second stage; on the contrary, he runs the entire distance without relation to the speed of the turtle, or to that of a lazy bear that might happen to be moving along the same course. The movement does not take place in one place or in another, but rather from one place toward another: the movement is precisely the passing from one place to another, and not a sequence of acts in different places.

Logos and Plato.

It is important to keep in mind that our purpose here is not to write a history of philosophy but rather to set forth as clearly as possible the Aristotelian concept of art as an imitation of nature, and to clarify what kind of nature it is, what kind of imitation, and what kind of art. This is why we have passed so lightly over many thinkers. Socrates, too, must suffer from this superficial treatment, since we want to establish only his concept of *logos*. For him, the real world needed to be conceptualized in the manner of the geometers. In nature there is an infinity of forms which are similar to a form generally designated as a triangle: thus the concept, the logos, of triangle is established; it is the geometrical figure having three sides and three angles. An infinity of real objects can thus be conceptualized. There exists, too, an infinite number of forms of objects that resemble the square, the circle, the polyhedron; therefore, the concepts of polyhedron, sphere, and square are established. The same should be done, Socrates said, with the logos of moral value in order to conceptualize courage, good, love, tolerance, etcetera.

Plato uses the Socratic idea of logos and goes beyond:

1. The idea is the intuitive vision we have, and precisely because it is intuitive, it is "pure": there is not in reality any perfect triangle, but the idea we have of the triangle (not of this or that triangle, that we can see in reality, but of the triangle "in general"); that idea is perfect. People who love, realize the act of love, but always imperfectly; what is perfect is the idea of love. All ideas are perfect; all the concrete things of reality are imperfect.

2. Ideas are the essence of things existing in the world perceptible to the senses; ideas are indestructible, immovable, immutable, timeless, and eternal.

3. Knowledge consists in elevating ourselves, through dialectics — that is, through the debate of ideas posed and counterposed, of ideas and the negations of those same ideas, which are other ideas — from the world of sensible reality to the world of eternal ideas. This ascent is knowledge.

What is the Meaning of "Imitation"?

This brings us back to Aristotle (384-322 B.C.), who rejects Plato:

1. Plato only multiplied the beings who for Parmenides were a single being; for him they are infinite, because the ideas are infinite.
2. The mataxis, that is, the participation of one world in another, is unintelligible; in truth, what has the world of perfect ideas to do with the imperfect world of real things? Is there movement from one to the other? If so, how does it take place?

Though Aristotle rejects Plato's system, he also utilizes it, introducing some new concepts: "substance" is the indissoluble unity of "matter" and "form." "Matter," in turn, is what constitutes substance; the matter of a tragedy is the words that constitute it; the matter of a statue is the marble. "Form" is the sum of the predicates we can attribute to a thing; it is all we can say about that thing. Each thing comes to be what it is (a statue, a book, a house, a tree) because its matter receives a form that gives meaning and purpose to it. This conceptualization confers on Platonic thought the dynamic characteristic that it lacked. The world of ideas does not coexist side by side with the world of reality, but rather the ideas (here called form) are the dynamic principle of matter. In the last analysis, reality for Aristotle is not a copy of ideas, though indeed it tends to perfection. It has in itself the moving force that will take it to that perfection. Man tends to health, to perfect bodily proportion, etc., and men as a whole tend to the perfect family, to the State. Trees tend to the perfection of the tree, that is, to the Platonic idea of a tree. Love tends to the perfect Platonic love. Matter, for Aristotle, is pure potential, and form is pure act; the movement of things toward perfection is therefore what he called "the enactment of potential," the passage from pure matter to pure form.

Our concern here is to insist on one point: for Aristotle, things themselves, by their own virtues (by their form, their moving force, by the enactment of their potential), tend to perfection. There are not two worlds; there is no mataxis: the world of perfection is yearning, a movement which develops matter toward its final form.

Therefore, what did "imitate" mean for Aristotle? To re-create that internal movement of things toward their perfection. Nature was for him this movement itself and not things already made, finished, visible. Thus "to imitate" has nothing to do with improvisation or "realism," and for this reason Aristotle could say that the artist must imitate men "as they should be" and not as they are.

What, then, is the Purpose of Art and Science?

If the things themselves tend to perfection, if perfection is immanent to all things and not transcendent, what, then, is the purpose of art and science?

Nature, according to Aristotle, tends to perfection, which does not mean that it always attains it. The body tends to health, but it can become ill; men in the aggregate tend to the perfect State, but wars can occur. Thus nature has certain ends in view, states of perfection toward which it tends — but sometimes nature fails. From this follows the purpose of art and science: by "re-creating the creative principle" of things, they correct nature where it has failed.

Here are some examples: the body "would tend" to resist rain, wind, and sun, but it does not in fact do so since the skin is not sufficiently resistant. Thus we invent the art of weaving and the manufacture of fabrics to protect the skin. The art of architecture constructs buildings and bridges, so that men can have shelter and cross rivers; medical science prepares medications for organs that have ceased to function as they should. Politics likewise tends to correct the faults that men have, even though they all tend to the perfect communal life.

That is the purpose of art and science: to correct the faults of nature, by using the suggestions of nature itself.

Major Arts and Minor Arts

The arts and sciences do not exist in isolation, without relation to each other, but on the contrary, are all interrelated according to the activity characteristic of each. They are also, in a certain way, arranged hierarchically according to the greater or lesser magnitude of their fields of action. The major arts are subdivided into minor arts, and each one of the latter deals with specific elements that compose the former.

Thus, the raising of horses is an art, as is also the work of the blacksmith. These arts, together with others — such as that of the man who makes leather goods, etc. — constitute a greater art, which is the art of equitation. The latter, in turn, joins with other arts — such as the art of topography, the art of strategy, etc. — to make up the art of war, and so on. Always a group of arts combines to form a more ample, greater, more complex art.

Another example: the art of manufacturing paints, the art of manufacturing paint brushes, the art of preparing the best canvas, the art of the combination of colors, etc., together constitute the art of painting.

So then, if there are minor arts and major arts, the latter being the ones that contain the former, there will be therefore a sovereign art, which will contain all the other arts and sciences, and whose field of action and concern will include all the fields of action of all the other arts and all the other sciences. This sovereign art, of course, will be the one whose laws rule over the relations among men in their totality. That is, Politics.

Nothing is alien to Politics, because nothing is alien to the superior art that rules the relations among men.

Medicine, war, architecture, etc. — minor and major arts, all without exception — are subject to, and make up, that sovereign art.

Thus we have established that nature tends toward perfection, that the arts and sciences correct nature in all its faults, and at the same time are interrelated under the domain of a sovereign art which deals with all men, with all they do, and all that is done for them: Politics.

What does Tragedy Imitate?

Tragedy imitates human acts. Human acts, not merely human activities. For Aristotle, man's soul was composed of a rational part and of another, irrational part. The irrational soul could produce certain activities such as eating, walking or performing any physical movement without greater significance than the physical act itself. Tragedy, on the other hand, imitated solely man's actions, determined by his rational soul.

Man's rational soul can be divided into:

      (a) faculties
      (b) passions
      (c) habits

A *faculty* is everything man is able to do, even though he may not do it. Man, even if he does not love, is able to love; even if he does not hate, he is able to hate; even if a coward, he is capable of showing courage. Faculty is pure potentiality and is immanent to the rational soul.

But, even though the soul has all the faculties, only some of them attain realization. These are the passions. A *passion* is not merely a "possibility," but a concrete fact. Love is a passion once it is expressed as such. As long as it is simply a possibility it will remain a faculty. A passion is an "enacted" faculty, a faculty that becomes a concrete act.

Not all passions serve as subject matter for tragedy. If a man, in a given moment, happens to exert a passion, that is not an action worthy of tragedy. It is necessary that that passion be constant in the man; that is, that by its repeated exertion it has become a *habit*. Thus we conclude that tragedy imitates man's actions, but only those produced by the habits of his rational soul. Animal activity is excluded, as well as the faculties and passions that have not become habitual.

To what end is a passion, a habit, exerted? What is the purpose of man? Each part of man has a purpose: the hand grabs, the mouth eats, the leg walks, the brain thinks, etc.; but as a whole being, what purpose does man have? Aristotle answers; the good is the aim of all man's actions. It is not an abstract idea of good, but rather the concrete good, diversified in all the different sciences and the different arts which deal with particular ends. Each human action, therefore, has an end limited to that action, but all actions as a whole have as their purpose the supreme good of man. What is the supreme good of man? Happiness!

Thus far we are able to say that tragedy imitates man's actions, those of his rational soul, directed to the attainment of his supreme end, happiness. But in order to understand which actions they are, we have to know first what happiness is.

What is Happiness?

The types of happiness, says Aristotle, are three: one that derives from material pleasures, another from glory, and a third from virtue.

For the average person, happiness consists in possessing material goods and enjoying them. Riches, honors, sexual and gastronomic pleasures, etc. — that is happiness. For the Greek philosopher, human happiness on this level differs very little from the happiness that animals can also enjoy. This happiness, he says, does not deserve to be studied in tragedy.

On a second level, happiness is glory. Here man acts according to his own virtue, but his happiness consists in the recognition of his actions by others. Happiness is not in the virtuous behavior itself, but in the fact that that behavior is recognized by others. Man, in order to be happy, needs the approval of others.

Finally, the superior level of happiness is that of the man who acts virtuously and asks no more. His happiness consists in acting in a virtuous manner, whether others recognize him or not. This is the highest degree of happiness: the virtuous exercise of the rational soul.

Now we know that tragedy imitates the actions of the rational soul — passions transformed into habits — of the man in search of happiness, which is to say, virtuous behavior. Very well. But now we need to know what is meant by "virtue."

And What is Virtue?

Virtue is the behavior most distant from the possible extremes of behavior in any given situation. Virtue cannot be found in the extremes: both the man who voluntarily refuses to eat and the glutton harm their health. This is not virtuous behavior; to eat with moderation is. The absence of physical exercise, as well as the too violent exercise, ruins the body; moderate physical exercise constitutes virtuous behavior. The same is true of the moral virtues. Creon thinks only of the good of the State, while Antigone thinks only of the good of the Family and wishes to bury her dead, traitorous brother. The two behave in a non-virtuous manner, for their conduct is extreme. Virtue would be found somewhere in the middle ground. The man who gives himself to all pleasures is a libertine, but the one who flees from all pleasures is an insensitive person. The one who confronts all dangers is foolhardy, but he who runs from all dangers is a coward.

Virtue is not exactly the average, for a soldier's courage is much closer to temerity than to cowardice. Nor does virtue exist in us "naturally"; it is necessary to learn it. The things of nature lack man's ability to acquire habits. The rock cannot fall upward nor can fire burn downward. But we can cultivate habits which will allow us to behave virtuously.

Nature, still according to Aristotle, gives us faculties, and we have the power to change them into actions (passions) and habits.

The one who practices wisdom becomes wise, he who practices justice becomes just, and the architect acquires his virtue as an architect by constructing buildings. Habits, not faculties! Habits, not merely ephemeral passions!

Aristotle goes farther and states that the formation of habits should begin in childhood and that a youth cannot practice politics because he needs first to learn all the virtuous habits taught by his elders, the legislators who instruct the citizens in virtuous habits.

Thus we know now that vice is extreme behavior and virtue is behavior characterized neither by excess nor deficiency. But if any given behavior is to be seen as either vicious or virtuous, it must fulfill four indispensable conditions: willfulness, freedom, knowledge, and constancy. These terms call for explanation. But let us bear in mind what we already know: that for Aristotle tragedy imitates the actions of man's rational soul (habitual passions) as he searches for happiness, which consists in virtuous behavior. Little by little our definition is becoming more complex.

Necessary Characteristics of Virtue

A man can behave in a totally virtuous manner and, in spite of that, not be considered virtuous; or he may behave in a vicious manner and not be considered vicious. In order to be considered virtuous or vicious, human action must meet four conditions.

First Condition: Willfulness.

Willfulness excludes the accidental. That is, man acts because he decides to act voluntarily, by his will and not by accident.

One day a mason put a stone on a wall in such a way that a strong wind blew it down. A pedestrian happened to be passing by, and the rock fell on him. The man died. His wife sued the mason, but the latter defended himself by saying that he had not committed any crime since he had not had the intention of killing the pedestrian. That is, his behavior was not vicious — he merely had an accident. But the judge did not accept this defense and found him guilty based on the fact that there was no willfulness in causing the death, but there was in placing the stone in a position such that it could fall and cause a death. In this respect there was willfulness.

If man acts because he wishes to, there we find virtue or vice. If his action is not determined by his will, one can speak neither of vice nor virtue. The one who does good without being aware of it is not for that a good person. Nor is he bad who causes harm involuntarily.

Second Condition: Freedom.

Here, exterior coercion is excluded. If a man commits an evil act because someone forces him with a gun to his head, one cannot in this case speak of vice. Virtue is free behavior, without any sort of exterior pressure.

In this case, too, a story is told — this time of a woman who, on being abandoned by her lover, decided to kill him, and so she did. Taken to court, she declared in her defense that she had not acted freely: her irrational passion forced her to commit the crime. According to her, there was no guilt here, no crime.

As before, the judge disagreed, ruling that passion is an integral part of a person, part of one's soul. Though there is no freedom when coercion comes from without, acts based upon inner impulse must be regarded as freely undertaken. The woman was condemned.

Third Condition: Knowledge.

It is the opposite of ignorance. The person who acts has before him an option whose terms he knows. In court a drunken criminal asserted that he had committed no crime because he was not conscious of what he was doing when he killed another man, and was therefore ignorant of his own actions. Also in this case, the drunk was condemned. Before he started drinking he had full knowledge that the alcohol was going to lead him to a state of unconsciousness; therefore he was guilty of letting himself fall into a state in which he lost consciousness of what he was doing.

In relation to this third condition of virtuous behavior, the conduct of characters such as Othello and Oedipus may seem questionable. With regard to both, we find discussions of the existence or nonexistence of knowledge (on which their virtue or vice would hinge). To my way of thinking the argument can be resolved as follows. Othello does not know the truth; this is correct. Iago lies to him about the infidelity of Desdemona, his wife, and Othello, blind with jealousy, kills her. But the tragedy of Othello goes far beyond a simple murder: his tragic flaw (and soon we will discuss the concept of *hamartia,* tragic flaw) is not that of having killed Desdemona. Nor is this habitual behavior.

But what indeed is a habit is his constant pride and his unreflective temerity. In several moments of the play Othello tells how he flung himself against his enemies, how he acted without reflecting upon the consequences of his actions. This, or his excessive pride, is the cause of his misfortune. And of these qualities, Othello is fully conscious, has full knowledge.

Also in the case of Oedipus, one must ask, what is his true flaw (hamartia)? His tragedy does not consist in having killed his father or married his mother. Those are not habitual acts either, and habit is one of the basic characteristics of virtuous or vicious behavior. But if we read the play with care, we will see that Oedipus, in all the important moments of his life, reveals his extraordinary pride, his arrogance, the vanity which leads him to believe that he is superior to the gods themselves. It is not the Moirai, (the Fates) that lead him to his tragic end; he himself, by his own decision, moves toward his misfortune. It is intolerance that causes him to kill an old man, who happens to be his father, because the latter did not treat him with the proper respect at a crossroads. And when he deciphers the enigma of the Sphinx, once more it is because of pride that he accepts the throne of Thebes and the hand of the Queen, a woman old enough to be his mother. And she really was! A person to whom the oracles (a kind of "voodoo witch doctor" or "seer" of the time) had said that he was going to marry his own mother and kill his own father would have to be a little careful and abstain from killing men old enough to be his father or marrying women old enough to be his mother. Why did he not exercise such care? Because of pride, haughtiness, intolerance, because he believed himself to be a worthy adversary of the gods. These are his flaws, his vices. To know or not the identity of Jocasta and Laius is secondary. Oedipus himself, when he recognizes his error, acknowledges these facts.

We conclude, therefore, that the third condition present in virtuous behavior consists in the agent's knowing the true terms of the option. He who acts in ignorance practices neither virtue nor vice.

Fourth Condition: Constancy.

Since virtues and vices are habits, not merely passions, it is necessary that virtuous or vicious behavior also be constant. All the heroes of the Greek tragedies act consistently in the same

manner. When the tragic flaw of the character consists precisely
in his incoherence, that character must be introduced as coher-
ently incoherent. Once more, neither accident nor chance characterize vice and virtue.

Thus those whom tragedy imitates are the virtuous men who,
upon acting, show willfulness, freedom, knowledge, and constancy. These are the four conditions necessary for the exercise
of virtue, which is man's way to happiness. But is virtue one, or
are there different degrees of virtue?

The Degrees of Virtue

Each art, each science, has its corresponding virtue, because each has its own end, its own good. The virtue of the horseman is to ride a horse well; the virtue of the ironsmith is to manufacture good iron tools. The virtue of the artist is to create a perfect work of art. That of the physician is to restore the health of the sick. That of the legislator is to make perfect laws that will bring happiness to the citizens.

While it is true that each art and each science has its own virtue, it is also true as we have already seen, that all the arts and all the sciences are interdependent and that some are superior to others, to the extent by which they are more complex than others and study or include larger sectors of human activity. Of all the arts and sciences, the sovereign art and science is Politics, because nothing is alien to it. Politics has for its field of study the totality of the relationships of the totality of men. Therefore the greatest good — the attainment of which would entail the greatest virtue — is the political good.

Tragedy imitates those actions of man which have the good as their goal; but it does not imitate actions which have minor ends, of secondary importance. Tragedy imitates actions that are directed toward the highest goal, the political good. And what is the political good? There is no doubt: the highest good is the political one, and the political good is justice!

What is Justice?

In the *Nicomachaean Ethics*, Aristotle proposes to us (and we accept) the principle that the just is that which is equal, and the unjust that which is unequal. In any division, the people that are equal should receive equal parts and those who (by any criterion) are unequal should receive unequal parts. Up to here we are in agreement. But we must define the criteria of inequality, because no one will want to be unequal in an inferior sense while all will want to be unequal in a superior one.

Aristotle himself was opposed to the *talion law* (an eye for an eye, a tooth for a tooth) because, he said, if the people were not equal, their eyes and teeth would not be equal either. Thus one would have to ask: whose eye for whose eye? If it was a master's eye for a slave's eye, it did not seem right to Aristotle, because for him those eyes were not equal in value. If it was a man's tooth for a woman's tooth, neither did Aristotle find here an equivalent value.

Then our philosopher utilizes an apparently honest argument to determine criteria of equality to which no one can object. He asks, should we begin with ideal, abstract principles and descend to reality or, on the contrary, should we look at concrete reality and from there ascend toward the principles? Far from any romanticism, he answers: obviously we should start with concrete reality. We must examine empirically the real, existing inequalities and upon them base our criteria of inequality.

This leads us to accept as "just" the *already existing* inequalities. For Aristotle, therefore, justice is already contained in reality itself as it is. He does not consider the possibility of *transforming the already existing inequalities*, but simply accepts them. And for this reason he decides that since free men and slaves do exist in reality (abstract principles do not matter), that will be the first criterion of inequality. To be a man is *more* and to be a woman is *less* — this is shown by concrete reality, according to Aristotle. Thus free men would rank highest; then would come free women, followed by male slaves, with the poor female slaves at the bottom.

That was Athenian democracy, which was based on the supreme value of "freedom." But not all societies were based on that same value; the oligarchies, for example, were based on the supreme value of wealth. There the men who owned more were considered superior to those who had less. Always starting with reality as it is. . . .

Thus we come to the conclusion that justice is not equality: justice is proportionality. And the criteria of proportionality are given by the political system actually in force in a particular city. Justice will always be proportionality, but the criteria which determine the latter will vary depending upon whether the system is a democracy, an oligarchy, a dictatorship, a republic, or other.

And how are the criteria of inequality established so that all become aware of them? Through laws. And who makes the laws? If the inferior human beings (women slaves, the poor) made them, they would, according to Aristotle, make inferior laws just as their authors are inferior. In order to have superior laws, it is necessary that they be made by superior beings: free men, wealthy men. . . .

The body of laws of a city, of a country, is put together and systematized in a constitution. The constitution, therefore, is the expression of the political good, the maximum expression of justice.

Finally, with the help of the *Nicomachaean Ethics*, we can arrive at a clear conclusion regarding what tragedy is for Aristotle. Its widest and most complete definition would be the following:

Tragedy imitates the actions of man's rational soul, his passions turned into habits, in his search for happiness, which consists in virtuous behavior, remote from the extremes, whose supreme good is justice and whose maximum expression is the Constitution.

In the final analysis, happiness consists in obeying the laws. This is Aristotle's message, clearly spelled out.

For those who make the laws, all is well. But what about those who do not make them? Understandably, they rebel, not wishing to accept the criteria of inequality provided by present reality, since they are criteria subject to modification, as is reality itself. In those cases, says the philosopher, sometimes war is necessary.

In What Sense can Theater Function as an Instrument for Purification and Intimidation?

We have seen that the population of a city is not *uniformly* content. If there is inequality, no one wants it to be to his disadvantage. It is necessary to make sure that all remain, if not uniformly satisfied, at least uniformly passive with respect to those criteria of inequality. How to achieve this? Through the many forms of repression: politics, bureaucracy, habits, customs — and Greek tragedy.

This statement may seem somewhat daring, but it is nothing more than the truth. Of course, the system presented by Aristotle in his *Poetics,* the functional system of tragedy (and all the forms of theater which to this day follow its general mechanism) is not *only* a system of repression. Other, more "esthetic," factors clearly enter into it. And there are many other apsects that ought likewise to be taken into account. But it is important to consider especially this fundamental aspect: its repressive function.

And why is the repressive function the fundamental aspect of the Greek tragedy and of the Aristotelian system of tragedy? Simply because, according to Aristotle, the principle aim of tragedy is to provoke catharsis.

The Ultimate Aim of Tragedy

The fragmentary nature of the *Poetics* has obscured the solid connection existing among its parts, as well as the hierarchy of the parts within the context of the whole. Only this fact explains why marginal observations, of little or no importance, have been taken to be central concepts of Aristotelian thought. For example, when dealing with Shakespeare or the medieval theater, it is very common to decide that such and such a play is not Aristotelian because it does not obey the "law of the three unities." Hegel's objection to this view is contained in his *The Philosophy of Fine Art:*

> The inalterability of one exclusive *locale* of the action proposed belongs to the type of those rigid rules which the French in particular have deduced from classic tragedy and the critique of Aristotle thereupon. As a matter of fact, Artistotle merely says that the duration of the tragic action should not exceed at the most the length of a day. He does not mention the unity of place at all. . . .[2]

The disproportionate importance that is given to this "law" is incomprehensible, since it has no more validity than would the statement that only the works that contain a prologue, five episodes and choral chants, and an exode are Aristotelian. The essence of Aristotelian thought cannot reside in structural aspects such as these. To emphasize these minor aspects is, in effect, to compare the Greek philosopher to the modern and abundant professors of dramaturgy, especially the Americans, who are no more than cooks of theatrical menus. They study the typical reactions of certain chosen audiences and from there extract conclusions and rules regarding how the perfect work should be written (equating perfection to box office success).

Aristotle, on the contrary, wrote a completely organic poetics, which is the reflection, in the field of tragedy and poetry, of all his philosophical contribution; it is the practical and concrete application of that philosophy specifically to poetry and tragedy.

For this reason, every time we find imprecise or fragmentary statements, we should immediately consult other texts written by the author. S. H. Butcher does precisely this, with crystal clear results, in his book *Aristotle's Theory of Poetry and Fine Art*.[3] He tries to understand the *Poetics* from the perspective of the *Metaphysics, Politics, Rhetoric*, and above all, the three *Ethics*. To him we owe mainly the clarification of the concept of catharsis.

Nature tends toward certain ends; when it fails to achieve those objectives, art and science intervene. Man, as part of nature, also has certain ends in view: health, gregarious life in the State, happiness, virtue, justice, etc. When he fails in the achievement of those objectives, the art of tragedy intervenes. This correction of man's actions is what Aristotle calls *catharsis*.

Tragedy, in all its qualitative and quantitative aspects, exists as a function of the effect it seeks, catharsis. All the unities of tragedy are structured around this concept. It is the center, the essence, the purpose of the tragic system. Unfortunately, it is also the most controversial concept. Catharsis is correction: what does it correct? Catharsis is purification: what does it purify?

Butcher helps us with a parade of opinions of such illustrious people as Racine, Milton, and Jacob Bernays.

Racine.

In tragedy, he wrote:

the passions are shown only to reveal all the disorder of which they are the cause; and vice is always painted with colors that make us know and hate the deformity . . . this is what the first tragic poets had in mind, more than anything else. Their theater was a school where the virtues were taught fully as well as in the philosopher's schools. For this reason Aristotle wanted to provide rules for the dramatic poem; . . . It is to be desired that our works should be as solid and as full of useful instructions as the ones of those poets.[4]

As we see, Racine emphasizes the doctrinal, moral aspect of tragedy; and this is fine, but there is one correction to be made: Aristotle did not advise the tragic poet to portray vicious characters. The tragic hero should suffer a radical change in the course of his life — from happiness to adversity — but this should happen not as a consequence of vice, but rather as a result of some error or weakness (see Chapter 13 of the *Poetics*). Soon we shall examine the nature of this *hamartia*.

It is necessary to understand also that the presentation of the error of weakness was not designed to make the spectator, in his immediate perception of it, feel repugnance or hatred. On the contrary, Aristotle suggested that the mistake or weakness be treated with some understanding. Almost always the state of "fortune" in which the hero is found at the beginning of the tragedy is due precisely to this fault and not to his virtues. Oedipus is King of Thebes because of a weakness in his character, that is, his pride. And indeed the efficacy of a dramatic process would be greatly diminished if the fault were presented from the beginning as despicable, the error as abominable. It is necessary, on the contrary, to show them as acceptable in order to destroy them later through the theatrical, poetic processes. Bad playwrights in every epoch fail to understand the enormous efficacy of the transformations that take place before the spectators' eyes. Theater is change and not simple presentation of what exists: it is becoming and not being.

Jacob Bernays.

In 1857, Bernays proposed an intriguing theory: the word "catharsis" would be a medical metaphor, a purgation which denotes the pathological effect on the soul, analogous to the effect of medicine on the body. Basing his argument on the definition of tragedy given by Aristotle ("imitation of human actions that excite pity or fear"), Bernays concludes that simply because these emotions are found in the hearts of all men, the act of exciting offers, afterward, a pleasant relaxation. This hypothesis seems to find confirmation in Aristotle himself, who declares that "pity is occasioned by undeserved misfortune, and fear by that of one like ourselves . . ." (Chapter 13). (We will soon examine the meaning of the word "empathy," which is based on those two emotions.)

The feelings stimulated by the spectacle, adds Bernays, are not removed in a permanent or definitive manner. But they remain calm for a certain time and all the system can rest. The stage thus offers harmless and pleasant discharge for the instincts that demand satisfaction and that can be tolerated much more easily in the fiction of the theater than in real life.[5]

Bernays, therefore, permits the supposition that perhaps the purgation does not refer only to the emotions of pity and fear, but also to certain "non-social" or socially forbidden instincts. Butcher himself, trying to understand what is the object of the purgation (that is, of what is one purged?), adds his own belief that it is the pity and terror we bring with us in our real life or, at least, those elements in our life which are disturbing.[6]

Is this clear? Perhaps that of which one is purged is not the emotions of pity or fear, but something contained in those emotions, or mixed with them. We must determine the identity of this foreign body which is eliminated by the cathartic process. In this case, pity and fear would only be part of the mechanism of expulsion and not its object. Here would reside the political significance of tragedy.

In Chapter XIX of the *Poetics* we read: "The Thought of the personages is shown in everything to be effected by their language — in every effort to prove or disprove, to arouse emotion (pity, fear, anger, and the like), . . ." We ask why purgation should not have been dealt with before in relation to "like" emotions such as hatred, envy, pride, partiality in worship of the gods and in the obedience to laws, etc.? Why choose pity and fear? Why does Aristotle explain the obligatory presence of these emotions only?

Analyzing some of the tragic characters, we see that they may be guilty of many ethical errors, but we can hardly say that any of them manifest either an excess or lack of pity or fear. It is never there that their virtue fails. Those emotions indeed play so little part that they cannot even be considered a characteristic common to all tragic characters.

It is not in the tragic characters that pity and fear manifest themselves — but rather in the *spectators. Through those emotions the spectators are linked to the heroes.* We must keep this clearly in mind: the spectators are linked to the heroes, *basically,* through the emotions of pity and fear, because, as Aristotle says, something *undeserved* happens to a character that *resembles ourselves.*

Let us clarify this a little more. Hippolytus loves all the gods intensely, and this is good, but he does not love the goddess of love, and this is bad. We feel pity because Hippolytus is destroyed in spite of all his good qualities, and fear because perhaps we are liable to criticism for the same reason of not loving all the gods, as the laws require. Oedipus is a great king, the people love him; his government is perfect, and for this reason we feel pity that such a wonderful person is destroyed for having one fault, pride, which perhaps we also have: hence our fear. Creon defends the right of the State and seeing that he has to bear the death of his wife and son causes pity in us because, together with all the virtues he possesses, he has the fault of seeing only the good of the State and not that of the Family; this one-sidedness could also be a fault of ours, hence the fear.

Once again, let us remember the relationship between the virtues and the fortune of the characters, ending with their downfall: Because of haughtiness and pride Oedipus becomes a great king; because he scorns the goddess of love, Hippolytus loves the other gods more intensely; and by caring excessively for the good of the State, Creon was in the beginning a great chieftain, at the peak of happiness.

We conclude, therefore, that pity and fear are the minimal specific form linking the spectator and the character. But these emotions are in no way the objects of purification (purgation). Rather, they are purified of something else which, at the end of the tragedy, ceases to exist.

Milton.

"Tragedy . . . said by Aristotle to be of power, by raising pity and fear, or terror, to purge the mind of those and such-like passions; that is to temper or reduce them to just measure with a kind of delight stirred up by reading or seeing those passions well imitated." Up to here, Milton adds very little to what has already been said; but something better follows: ". . . in physick medicine, things of melancholick hue and quality are used against melancholy, sour against sour, salt to remove salt humours."[7] In effect, it is a kind of homeopathy — certain emotions or passions curing analogous, but not identical, emotions or passions.

Besides his study of the views of Milton, Bernays and Racine, Butcher goes to Aristotle's own *Politics* to find the explanation of the word *catharsis* which is not to be found in the *Poetics*. Catharsis is utilized there to denote the effect caused by a certain kind of music on patients possessed by a given type of religious fervor. The treatment "consisted in applying movement to cure movement, in soothing the internal trouble of the mind by a wild and restless music." According to Aristotle, the patients subjected to that treatment returned to their normal state, as if they had undergone a medical or purgative treatment — that is, cathartic.[8]

In this example we verify that through "homeopathic" means (savage music to cure savage interior rhythms), the religious fervor was cured by means of an analogous exterior effect. The cure was brought about through the stimulus. As in the tragedy, the character's fault is initially presented as cause of his happiness — the fault is stimulated.

Butcher adds that, according to Hippocrates, catharsis meant removal of a painful or disturbing element in the organism, purifying in this way what remains, free finally of the eliminated extraneous matter. Butcher concludes that applying the same definition to tragedy, one will arrive at the conclusion that "pity and fear" in real life contain a morbid or disturbing element. During the process of tragic excitation this element, whatever it may be, is eliminated. "As the tragic action progresses, when the tumult of the mind, first roused, has afterward subsided, the lower forms of emotion are found to have been transmuted into higher and more refined forms."[9]

This reasoning is correct and we can accept it totally, except for its insistent attribution of impurities to the emotions of pity and fear. The impurity exists, no doubt, and it is in fact the object of purgation in the character's mind, or as Aristotle would say, in his very *soul*. But Aristotle does not speak of the existence of pure or impure pity, pure or impure fear. The impurity is *necessarily distinct from* the emotions which will remain once the spectacle of the tragedy is ended. That extraneous matter — the eliminated impurity — can only be an emotion or passion other than the ones that remain. Pity and fear have never been vices or weaknesses or errors and, therefore, never needed to be eliminated or purged. On the other hand, in the *Ethics*, Aristotle points to numerous vices, errors, and weaknesses which do indeed deserve to be destroyed.

The impurity to be purged must undoubtedly be found among the latter. It must be something that threatens the individual's equilibrium, and consequently that of society. Something that is not virtue, that is not the greatest virtue, justice. And since all that is unjust is forseen in the laws, the impurity which the tragic process is destined to destroy is therefore something *directed against the laws*.

If we go back a little, we will be able to understand better the workings of tragedy. Our last definition was: "Tragedy imitates the actions of man's rational soul, his passions turned into habits, in his search for happiness, which consists in virtuous behavior . . . whose supreme good is justice and whose maximum expression is the Constitution."

We have also seen that nature tends toward certain ends, and when nature fails, art and science intervene to correct it.

We can conclude, therefore, that when man fails in his actions — in his virtuous behavior as he searches for happiness through the maximum virtue, which is obedience to the laws — the art of tragedy intervenes to correct that failure. How? Through purification, catharsis, through purgation of the extraneous, undesirable element which prevents the character from achieving his ends. This extraneous element is contrary to the law; it is a social fault, a political deficiency.

We are finally ready to understand how the tragic scheme works. But first, a short glossary may serve to simplify certain words which represent the elements we are going to assemble in order to clarify the coercive system of tragedy.

A Short Glossary of Simple Words

Tragic hero.

As Arnold Hauser explains in his *Social History of Art,* in the beginning, the theater was the chorus, the mass, the people.[10] They were the true protagonist. When Thespis *invented* the protagonist, he immediately "aristocratized" the theater, which existed before in its popular forms of mass manifestations, parades, feasts, etc. The protagonist-chorus dialogue was clearly a reflection of the aristocrat-people (commoners) dialogue. The tragic hero, who later begins to carry on a dialogue not only with the chorus but also with his peers (deuteragonist and tritagonist), was always presented as an example which should be followed in certain characteristics but not in others. The tragic hero appears when the State begins to utilize the theater for the political purpose of coercion of the people. It should not be forgotten that the State, directly or through certain wealthy patrons, paid for the theatrical productions.

Ethos.

The character acts and his performance presents two aspects: ethos and *dianoia*. The two together constitute the action developed by the character. They are inseparable. But for explanatory purposes we could say that ethos is the action itself, while dianoia is the justification of that action, the reasoning. Ethos would be the act itself and dianoia the thought that determines the act. But one should bear in mind that the reasoning is also action, and there can be no action, no matter how physical and limited it may be, that does not suppose a reason.

We can define ethos as the whole of the faculties, passions, and habits.

In the ethos of the tragic protagonist all tendencies must be good.

Except one.

All the passions, all the habits of the character must be good, with one exception. According to which criteria? According to constitutional criteria, which are those that systematize the laws; that is, according to political criteria, since politics is the sovereign art. Only one trait must be bad — only one passion, one habit, will be against the law. This bad characteristic is called *hamartia.*

Hamartia.

It is also known as the *tragic flaw.* It is the only "impurity" that exists in the character. Hamartia is the only thing that can and must be destroyed, so that the whole of the character's ethos may conform to the ethos of the society. In this confrontation of tendencies, of ethos, the hamartia causes the conflict: it is the only trait that is not in harmony with what society regards as desirable.

Empathy.

From the moment the performance begins, a relationship is established between the character, especially the protagonist, and the spectator. This relationship has well defined characteristics: the spectator assumes a passive attitude and delegates the power of action to the character. Since the character resembles us (as Aristotle indicates), we live *vicariously* all his stage experiences. Without acting, we feel that we are acting. We love and hate when the character loves and hates.

Empathy does not take place only with tragic characters: it is enough to see children very excited, watching a "Western" on television, or the sentimental looks of the public when, on the screen, the hero and the heroine exchange kisses. It is a case of pure empathy. Empathy makes us feel as if we ourselves are experiencing what is actually happening to others.

Empathy is an emotional relationship between character and spectator. A relationship which, as Aristotle suggests, can be basically one of pity and fear, but which can include other emotions as well: love, tenderness, desire (in the case of many movie stars and their fan clubs), etc.

Empathy takes place especially in relation to what the character *does* — that is, his ethos. But there is likewise an empathic relationship *dianoia* (the character's) — *reason* (the spectator's), which corresponds to *ethos-emotion*. The ethos stimulates emotion; the dianoia stimulates reason.

Clearly, the fundamental empathic emotions of pity and fear are evoked on the basis of an ethos which reveals good traits (hence pity for the character's destruction) and one bad trait, hamartia (hence fear, because we also possess it).

Now we are ready to return to the functioning of the tragic scheme.

How Aristotle's Coercive System
of Tragedy Functions

The spectacle begins. The tragic hero appears. The public establishes a kind of empathy with him.

The action starts. Surprisingly, the hero shows a flaw in his behavior, a hamartia; and even more surprising, one learns that it is by virtue of this same hamartia that the hero has come to his present state of happiness.

Through empathy, the same hamartia that the spectator may possess is stimulated, developed, activated.

Suddenly, something happens that changes everything. (Oedipus, for example, is informed by Teiresias that the murderer he seeks is Oedipus himself.) The character, who because of a hamartia had climbed so high, runs the risk of falling from those heights. This is what the *Poetics* classifies as *peripeteia*, a radical change in the character's destiny. The spectator, who up to then had his own hamartia stimulated, starts to feel a growing fear. The character is now on the way to misfortune. Creon is informed of the death of his son and his wife; Hippolytus cannot convince his father of his innocence, and the latter impells his son, unintentionally, to death.

Peripeteia is important because it lengthens the road from happiness to misfortune. The taller the palm tree, the greater the fall, says a popular Brazilian song. That way creates more impact.

The peripeteia suffered by the character is reproduced in the spectator as well. But it could happen that the spectator would follow the character empathically until the moment of the peripeteia and then detach himself at that point. In order to avoid that, the tragic character must also pass through what Aristotle calls *anagnorisis* — that is, through the recognition of his flaw as such and, by means of reasoning, the explanation of it. The hero accepts his error, hoping that, empathically, the spectator will also accept as bad his own hamartia. But the spectator has the great advantage of having erred only vicariously: he does not really pay for it.

Finally, so that the spectator will keep in mind the terrible consequences of committing the error not just vicariously but in actuality, Aristotle demands that tragedy have a terrible end, which he calls *catastrophe.* The happy end is not permitted, though the character's physical destruction is not absolutely required. Some die; others see their loved ones die. In any case, the catastrophe is always such that not to die is worse than death.

Those three interdependent elements (peripeteia, anagnorisis, catastrophe) have the ultimate goal of provoking catharsis in the spectator (as much or more than in the character); that is, their purpose is to produce a purgation of the hamartia, passing through three clearly defined stages:

First Stage: Stimulation of the hamartia; the character follows an ascending path toward happiness, accompanied empathically by the spectator. Then comes a moment of reversal: the character, with the spectator, starts to move from happiness toward misfortune; fall of the hero.

Second Stage: The character recognizes his error — *anagnorisis.* Through the empathic relationship *dianola-reason*, the spectator recognizes his own error, his own hamartia, his own anticonstitutional flaw.

Third Stage: Catastrophe; the character suffers the consequences of his error, in a violent form, with his own death or with the death of loved ones.

Catharsis: The spectator, terrified by the spectacle of the catastrophe, is purified of his hamartia.

Aristotle's coercive system can be shown graphically:

[handwritten marginal note:] Basic sequence of Forum theatre/Community theatre; heightened the loss due to such emphasise the actions through the character's hamartia

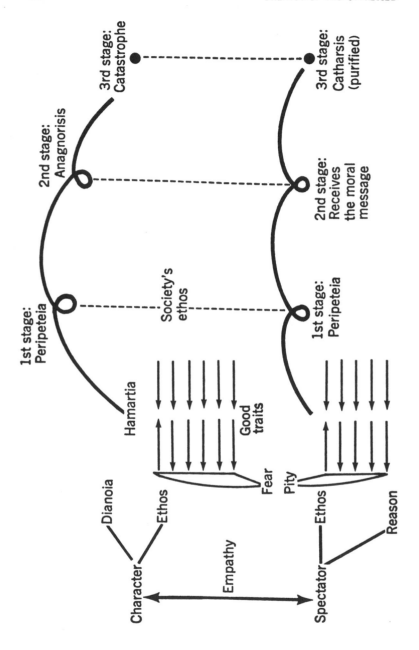

The words *"Amicus Plato, sed magis amicus veritas"* ("I am Plato's friend, but I am more of a friend of truth!") are attributed to Aristotle. In this we agree entirely with Aristotle: we are his friends, but we are much better friends of truth. He tells us that poetry, tragedy, theater have nothing to do with politics. But reality tells us something else. His own *Poetics* tells us it is not so. We have to be better friends of reality: all of man's activities — including, of course, all the arts, especially theater — are political. And theater is the most perfect artistic form of coercion.

Different Types of Conflict:
Hamartia and Social Ethos

As we have seen, Aristotle's coercive system of tragedy requires:

a) the creation of a conflict between the character's ethos and the ethos of the society in which he lives; something is not right!

b) the establishment of a relationship called empathy, which consists in allowing the spectator to be guided by the character through his experiences; the spectator — feeling as if he himself is acting — enjoys the pleasures and suffers the misfortunes of the character, to the extreme of thinking his thoughts.

c) that the spectator experience three changes of a rigorous nature: *peripeteia, anagnorisis,* and *catharsis;* he *suffers a blow* with regard to his fate (the action of the play), *recognizes the error* vicariously committed and *is purified of the antisocial characteristic* which he sees in himself.

This is the essence of the coercive system of tragedy. In the Greek theater the system functions as it is shown in our diagram; but in its essence, the system survived and has continued to be utilized down to our own time, with various modifications introduced by new societies. Let us analyze some of these modifications.

First Type: Hamartia Versus the Perfect
Social Ethos (classical type).

This is the most classical case studied by Aristotle. Consider again the example of Oedipus. The perfect social ethos is presented through the Chorus or through Teiresias in his long speech. The collision is head-on. Even after Teiresias has declared that the criminal is Oedipus himself, the latter does not accept it and continues the investigation on his own. Oedipus — the perfect man, the obedient son, the loving husband, the model father, the statesman without equal, intelligent, handsome, and sensitive — has nevertheless a tragic flaw: his pride! Through it he climbs to the peak of his glory, and through it he is destroyed. The balance is re-established with the catastrophe, with the terrifying vision of the protagonist's hanged mother-wife and his eyes torn out.

Second Type: Hamartia Versus Hamartia
Versus the Perfect Social Ethos.

The tragedy presents two characters who meet, two tragic heroes, each one with his flaw, who destroy each other before an ethically perfect society. This is the typical case of Antigone and Creon, both very fine persons in every way with the exception of their respective flaws. In these cases, the spectator must necessarily *empathize with both characters,* not only one, since the tragic process must purify him of two hamartias. A spectator who empathizes only with Antigone can be led to think that Creon possesses the truth, and vice versa. The spectator must purify himself of the "excess," whatever direction it takes — whether excess of love of the State to the detriment of the Family, or excess of love of the Family to the detriment of the good of the State.

Often, when the anagnorisis of the character is perhaps not enough to convince the spectator, the tragic author utilizes the direct reasoning of the Chorus, possessor of common sense, moderation, and other qualities.

In this case also the catastrophe is necessary in order to produce, through fear, the catharsis, the purification of evil.

Third Type: Negative Hamartia Versus
the Perfect Social Ethos.

This type is completely different from the two presented before. Here the ethos of the character is presented in a negative form; that is, he has all the faults and only a single virtue, and not as was taught by Aristotle, all the virtues and only one fault, flaw, or mistake of judgment. Precisely because he possesses that small and solitary virtue the character is saved, the catastrophe is avoided, and instead a happy end occurs.

It is important to note that Aristotle clearly objected to the happy end, but we should note, too, that the coercive character of his whole system is the true essence of his political *Poetics;* therefore, in changing a characteristic as important as the composition of the ethos of the character, the structural mechanism of the end of the work is inevitably changed also, in order to maintain the purgative effect.

This type of catharsis, produced by "negative hamartia versus the perfect social ethos," was often used in the Middle Ages. Perhaps the best known medieval drama is *Everyman.*

It tells the story of the character named Everyman, who when it comes time to die, tries to save himself, has a dialogue with Death, and analyzes all his past actions. Before Everyman and Death passes a whole series of characters who accuse Everyman and reveal the sins committed by him: the material goods, the pleasures, etc. Everyman finally recognizes all the sins he has committed, admits the complete absence of any virtue in his actions, but at the same time trusts in divine mercy. This faith is his only virtue. This faith and his repentance save him, for the greater glory of God. . . .

The anagnorisis (recognition of his sins) is practically accompanied by the birth of a new character, and the latter is saved. In tragedy, the acts of the character are irremediable; but in this type of drama, the acts of the character can be forgiven provided he decides to change his life completely and become a "new" character.

The idea of a new life (and this one is the forgiven life, since the sinning character ceases to be a sinner) can be seen clearly in *Condemned for Faithlessness (El condenado por desconfiado)* by Tirso de Molina. The hero, Enrique, has all the worst faults to be found in a person: he is a drunkard, murderer, thief, scoundrel — no defect, crime, or vice is alien to him. Wickedness that the Devil himself might envy. He has the most perverted ethos that dramatic art has ever invented. At his side is Pablo, the pure one, incapable of committing the slightest, most forgivable little sin, an immaculate spirit, insipid, empty, the image of perfection!

But something very strange happens to this pair which will cause their fate to be exactly the opposite of what one would expect. Enrique, the bad one, knows himself to be evil and a sinner, and never doubts that divine justice will condemn him to burn in the flames of the deepest and darkest corner of hell. And he accepts the divine wisdom and its justice. On the other hand, Pablo sins by wanting to keep himself pure. At every instant he wonders if God will truly realize that his life has been one of sacrifice and want. He ardently wishes to die and move immediately to heaven, so that he can possibly begin there a more pleasant life.

The two of them die, and to the surprise of some, the divine verdict is as follows: Enrique, in spite of all the crimes, robberies, drunkenness, treasons, etc., goes to heaven, because his firm belief in his punishment glorified God; Pablo, on the other hand, did not truly believe in God, since he doubted his salvation; therefore, he goes to hell with all his virtues.

That, in rough outline, is the play. Observed from the point of view of Enrique, it is clearly a case of a thoroughly evil ethos, possessing a single virtue. The exemplary effect is obtained through the happy end and not through the catastrophe. Observed from the point of view of Pablo, it is a conventional, classical, Aristotelian scheme. Everything in Pablo was virtue, with the exception of his tragic flaw — doubting God. For him there is indeed a catastrophe!

Fourth Type: Negative Hamartia Versus Negative Social Ethos.

The word "negative" is employed here in the sense of referring to a model that is the exact opposite of the original positive model — without reference to any moral quality. As, for instance, in a photographic negative, where all that is white shows up black and vice versa.

This type of ethical conflict is the essence of "romantic drama," and *Camille (La Dame aux camélias)* is its best example. The hamartia of the protagonist, as in the preceding case, displays an impressive collection of negative qualities, sins, errors, etc. On the other hand, the social ethos (that is, the moral tendencies, ethics) of the society — contrary to the preceding example (third type) — is here entirely in agreement with the character. All her vices are perfectly acceptable, and she would suffer nothing for having them.

In *Camille* we see a corrupted society, which accepts prostitution, and Marguerite Gauthier is the best prostitute — individual vice is defended and accepted by the vicious society. Her profession is perfectly acceptable, her house frequented by society's most respected men (considering that it is a society whose principal value is money, her house is frequented by financiers) . . . Marguerite's life is full of happiness! But, poor girl, all her faults are accepted, though not her only virtue. Marguerite falls in love. Indeed, she truly loves someone. Ah, no, not that. Society cannot permit it; it is a tragic flaw and must be punished.

Here, from the ethical point of view, a sort of triangle is established. Up to now we have analyzed conflicts in which the "social ethics" was the same for the characters as for the spectators; now a dichotomy is presented: the author wishes to show a social ethics accepted by the society portrayed on stage, but he himself, the author, does not share that ethics, and proposes another. The universe of the work is one, and our universe, or at least our momentary position during the spectacle, is another. Alexander Dumas (Dumas fils) says in effect: here you see what this society is like, and it is bad, but we are not like that, or we are not like that in our innermost being. Thus, Marguerite has all the virtues that society believes to be virtues; a prostitute must practice her profession of prostitute with dignity and efficiency. But Marguerite has a flaw which prevents her from practicing her profession well — she falls in love. How can a woman in love with *one* man serve with equal fidelity *all* men (all those who can pay)? Impossible. Therefore, falling in love, for a prostitute, is not a virtue but a vice.

But we, the spectators, who do not belong to the universe of the work, can say the exact opposite: a society which allows and encourages prostitution is a society which must be changed. Thus the triangle is established: to love, for us is a virtue, but in the universe of the work, it is a vice. And Marguerite Gauthier is destroyed precisely because of that vice (virtue).

Also in this kind of romantic drama, the catastrophe is inevitable. And the romantic author hopes that the spectator will be purified not of the tragic flaw of the hero, but rather of the whole ethos of society.

The same modification of the Aristotelian scheme is found in another romantic drama, *An Enemy of the People,* by Ibsen. Here again, the character, Dr. Stockman, embodies an ethos identical to that of the society in which he lives, a society based on profit, on money; but he also possesses a flaw: he is an honest man! This the society cannot tolerate. The powerful impact this work usually has stems from the fact that Ibsen shows (whether intentionally or not) that societies based on profit find it impossible to foster an "elevated" morality. Capitalism is fundamentally immoral because the search for profit, which is its essence, is incompatible with its official morality, which preaches superior human values, justice, etc.

Dr. Stockman is destroyed (that is, he loses his position in society, as does his daughter, who becomes an outcast in a competitive society) precisely because of his basic virtue, which is here considered vice, error, or tragic flaw.

*Fifth Type: Anachronistic Individual Ethos
Versus Contemporary Social Ethos.*

This is the typical case of Don Quixote: his social ethos is perfectly synchronized with the ethos of a society that no longer exists. This past society, now nonexistent, enters into a confrontation with the contemporary society and the resultant conflicts are inevitable. The anachronistic ethos of Don Quixote, knight errant and lordly Spanish hidalgo, cannot live peacefully in a time when the bourgeoisie is developing — the bourgeoisie which changes all values and for whom all things become money, as money comes to equal all things.

A variation of the "anachronistic ethos" is that of the "diachronic ethos": the character lives in a moral world made up of values which society honors in word but not in deed. In *José, from Birth to Grave,* the character, José da Silva, embodies all the values that the bourgeoisie claims as its own, and his misfortune comes precisely because he believes in those values and rules his life by them: a "self-made man," he works more than he has to, is devoted to his employers, avoids causing labor troubles, etc. In short, a character who follows *The Laws of Success* of Napoleon Hill, or *How to Win Friends and Influence People* of Dale Carnegie. That is tragedy! And what a tragedy!

Conclusion

Aristotle's coercive system of tragedy survives to this day, thanks to its great efficacy. It is, in effect, a powerful system of intimidation. The structure of the system may vary in a thousand ways, making it difficult at times to find all the elements of its structure, but the system will nevertheless be there, working to carry out its basic task: the purgation of all antisocial elements. Precisely for that reason, the system cannot be utilized by revolutionary groups *during* revolutionary periods. That is, while the social ethos is not clearly defined, the tragic scheme cannot be used, for the simple reason that the character's ethos will not find a clear social ethos that it can confront.

The coercive system of tragedy can be used before or after the revolution . . . but never during it!

In fact, only more or less stable societies, ethically defined, can offer a scale of values which would make it possible for the system to function. During a "cultural revolution," in which all values are being formed or questioned, the system cannot be applied. That is to say that the system, insofar as it structures certain elements which produce a determined effect, can be utilized by any society as long as it possesses a definite social ethos; for it to function, technically whether the society is feudal, capitalist, or socialist does not matter: what matters is that it have a universe of definite, accepted values.

On the other hand, an understanding of how the system functions often becomes difficult because one places himself in a false perspective. For example: the stories of "Western" movies are Aristotelian (at least, all the ones I have seen). But to analyze them it is necessary to regard them from the perspective of the bad man rather than from that of the "good guy," from the viewpoint not of the hero but of the villain.

A "Western" story begins with the presentation of a villain (bandit, horse thief, murderer, or whatever) who, precisely because of his vice or tragic flaw, is the uncontested boss, the richest or the most feared man of the neighborhood or city. He does all the evil he possibly can, and we empathize with him and vicariously we do the same evil — we kill, steal horses and chickens, rape young heroines, etc. Until, after our own hamartia has been stimulated, the moment of the *peripeteia:* the hero gains advantage in the fist fight or through endless shoot-outs and reestablishes order (social ethos), morality, and honest business relationships, after destroying *(catastrophe)* the bad citizen. What is left out here is the *anagnorisis,* and the villain is allowed to die without feeling regrets; in short, they finish him off with gunshots and bury him, while the townspeople celebrate with square dances. . . .

How often — remember? — our sympathy has been (in a certain way, empathy) more with the bad guy than with the good one! The "Westerns," like children's games, serve the Aristotelian purpose of purging all the spectator's aggressive tendencies.

This system functions to diminish, placate, satisfy, eliminate all that can break the balance — all, including the revolutionary, transforming impetus.

Let there be no doubt. Aristotle formulated a very powerful purgative system, the objective of which is to eliminate all that is not commonly accepted, including the revolution, before it takes place. His system appears in disguised form on television, in the movies, in the circus, in the theaters. It appears in many and varied shapes and media. But its essence does not change: it is designed to bridle the individual, to adjust him to what pre-exists. If this is what we want, the Aristotelian system serves the purpose better than any other; if, on the contrary, we want to stimulate the spectator to transform his society, to engage in revolutionary action, in that case we will have to seek another poetics!

General Notes

A. The distinctive qualities of the character are related to the denouement. A totally good character who comes to a happy end inspires neither pity nor terror, nor does he create a dynamics: the spectator observes him acting out his destiny, but there is an absence of drama.

Likewise, a totally bad character who ends up in catastrophe does not inspire pity, which is a necessary part of the mechanism of empathy.

A totally good character who ends in catastrophe is not a model either and, on the contrary, violates the sense of justice. This is the case of Don Quixote, who from the point of view of the ethics of Knighthood is totally good and nevertheless suffers a catastrophe which functions "exemplarily." It can be said that he is totally good, but that he adheres to an anachronistic moral code, which is in itself a tragic flaw. That is his hamartia.

A totally bad character who ends happily would be entirely contrary to the purposes of Greek tragedy and would stimulate evil instead of good.

Thus we have to conclude that the only possibilities are:
1) character with a flaw, ending in catastrophe;
2) character with a virtue, coming to a happy end;
3) character with a virtue, but insufficient, ending in catastrophe.

B. For Plato, reality is as if a man were imprisoned in a cell with a single, high window: the man would only be able to distinguish shadows of true reality. For this reason Plato argued against artists; they would be like prisoners who in their cells would paint the shadows which they mistake for reality — copies of copies, double corruption!

C. The *anagnorisis* is a fundamental and very important element of the system. It can be the recognition made by the character himself, and thus empathically this recognition is transferred to the spectator. But in any case, the recognition is made by the character with whom an empathic relationship exists. It is risky not to produce anagnorisis, or to do it poorly or insufficiently. One must remember that the spectator initially has his own flaw stimulated, and failure to understand the fact that it is a flaw will increase its destructive power.

It can also happen that the spectator will empathically follow the character until the peripeteia begins and will abandon him from that moment on. There is the danger and there the system can work in reverse!

Likewise, the non-destruction of the hamartia (happy end) can stimulate the spectator: if the character did the harm he did and nothing happened to him, then "nothing will happen to me either." This frees the spectator and stimulates him to do evil.

D. "Becoming and not being": Fundamental to the thought of Aristotle was becoming, not being. For him, "to become" meant not accidental appearance and disappearance, but instead the development of what already exists in a germinal state. The individual, concrete thing, is not an appearance but a proper, embryonic, existing reality.

E. For Aristotle, esthetic pleasure is given by the union of matter with a form which in the real world is foreign to it. This union of matter with a (foreign) form produces the esthetic pleasure. For example, to express joy not as in real life, but by means of a flute. That is how esthetic pleasure arises. Aristotle also insists that "the fine arts imitate men in action." The concept is ample and includes all that makes up the internal and essential activity, all the mental and spiritual life, or that reveals the personality. The external world can also be included but only in the measure to which it serves to express the internal action.

Can one achieve happiness in life? For Aristotle, yes, since to be happy is to live virtuously. A virtuous man can be an unfortunate but never an unhappy man.

Aristotle adds that in order to be happy a minimum of objective conditions is necessary, since happiness is not a moral disposition but rather is based on acts which are in fact carried out. With that we are in agreement.

Notes for Chapter 1

[1] Arnold Hauser, *The Social History of Art,* trans. Stanley Godman, 4 vols. (New York: Vintage Books, Inc., 1957), 1:83, 84-85, 87.

[2] G. W. F. Hegel, *The Philosophy of Fine Art,* trans. F. P. B. Osmaston, 4 vols. (London: G. Bell and Sons, Ltd., 1920), 4:257.

[3] S. H. Butcher, *Aristotle's Theory of Poetry and Fine Art,* 4th ed. (New York: Dover Publications, Inc., 1951).

[4] "Les passions n'y sont présentées aux yeux que pour montrer tout le désordre dont elles sont cause; et le vice y est peint partout avec des couleurs qui en font connaître et haïr la difformité . . . et c'est ce que les premiers poètes tragiques avaient en vue sur toute chose. Leur théâtre était une école où la vertu n'était pas moins bien enseignée que dans les écoles des philosophes. Aussi Aristote a bien voulu donner des règles due pòeme dramatique . . . Il serait à souhaiter que nos ouvrages fussent aussi solides et aussi pleins d'utiles instructions que ceux de ces poètes." Cited in Butcher, pp. 243-244 note.

[5] Butcher, p. 245.

[6] Butcher, pp. 252-54.

[7] Cited in Butcher, pp. 247-48.

[8] Butcher, pp. 248-49.

[9] Butcher, p. 254.

[10] Hauser, 1:86.

Machiavelli and the Poetics of *Virtù*

This essay was written in 1962 as an introduction to the performance of Mandragola, *a comedy by Machiavelli, produced by the Arena Theater of São Paulo in 1962-63 under my direction.*

In preparing this book I first thought of omitting the third part of this essay, which deals specifically with the play and its characters. It occurred to me, however, that the omission would result in a loss of continuity in the discussion. I also wanted to add some new sections, especially one on the "Metamorphoses of the Devil," but I feared that dwelling too long on some aspects of the general outline might work to the detriment of the whole. I must make clear that this essay does not intend to study exhaustively the profound transformations undergone by the theater under bourgeois direction. It attempts only to make an outline of those transformations. Every outline suffers from inadequacy, a danger of which I have been fully aware both before and after undertaking the task.

The Feudal Abstraction

According to Aristotle, as well as Hegel or Marx, art, in any of its modes, genres, or styles, always constitutes a sensorial way of transmitting certain kinds of knowledge — subjective or objective, individual or social, particular or general, abstract or concrete, super- or infrastructural. That knowledge, adds Marx, is revealed according to the perspective of the artist or of the social sector in which he is rooted, or which sponsors him, pays him, or consumes his work — especially that sector of society which holds the economic power, controlling with it all the other powers and establishing the directives of all creativity, be it artistic, scientific, philosophical, or any other. This sector is evidently interested in the transmission of that knowledge which helps it to maintain its power, if it already possesses it in an absolute form, or if not, helps it to conquer that power. This does not, however, prevent other sectors or classes from fostering also their own art, which translates the knowledge necessary to them, and in doing so are guided by their own perspective. But the dominant art will always be that of the dominant class, since it is the only class that possesses the means to disseminate it.

The theater, in particular, is determined by society much more stringently than the other arts, because of its immediate contact with the public, and its greater power to convince. That determination extends to the exterior presentation of the spectacle as well as the content itself of the ideas of the written text.

Regarding the exterior qualities, it is enough to bring to mind the great differences between the formal techniques of, for example, Shakespeare and Sheridan: the violence of the first and the gentleness of the second — the duels, the mutinies, the witchcraft and ghosts, on one hand, and, on the other, the petty intrigues, the innuendo, the structural complexity of the little plots. Faced with the violent, tumultuous Elizabethan audience, Sheridan would be ineffective, just as Shakespeare would be considered bloody and gross, a savage torturer of characters, by the spectators of Drury Lane in the second half of the eighteenth century.

As for the content, the examples that might be cited are less obvious, though the social influence can be verified without undue effort, as much on the billboards of São Paulo's theaters today as in Greek drama.

In his book *The Social History of Art*, while analyzing the social function of Greek tragedy, Arnold Hauser writes that "the externals of its presentation to the masses were democratic, but its content, the heroic sagas with their tragi-heroic outlook on life, was aristocratic. . . . It unquestionably propagates the standards of the great-hearted individual, the uncommon distinguished man [i.e., the aristocrat]. . . ." Hauser points out, too, that Athens was an "imperialistic democracy," whose numerous wars brought benefits only for the dominant sectors of society and whose only progress was that of gradually substituting an aristocracy of money for an aristocracy of blood. The State and the wealthy financed the production of tragedies and, therefore, would not permit the performance of plays whose content would run counter to State policy or to the interests of the governing classes.[1]

In the Middle Ages the control of theatrical production, exercised by the clergy and nobility, was even more effective, and the relations between feudalism and medieval art can easily be shown through the establishment of an ideal type of art — which, of course, need not explain all the particular cases, though many times perfect examples may be found.

The near self-sufficiency of each feudal manor, the social system of rigidly stratified estates, the insignificance — the almost total absence — of commerce must produce an art which, as Hauser shows, places no value on what is new, but rather attempts to preserve the old, the traditional. The Middle Ages lacked the idea of competition, which only appears later with individualism.[2]

The aims of feudal art were the same as those of the clergy and nobility: to immobilize society by perpetuating the existing system. Its principal characteristic was depersonalization, deindividualization, abstraction. The function of art was authoritarian, coercive, inculcating in the people a solemn attitude of religious respect for the status quo. It presented a static, stereotyped world, in which the generic and homogeneous prevailed. Transcendent values were of prime importance, while individual, concrete phenomena had no intrinsic value, serving only as symbols or signs.[3]

The Church itself simply tolerated and later utilized art as a mere vehicle for its ideas, dogmas, precepts, commandments, and decisions. The artistic means represented a concession made by the clergy to the ignorant masses, incapable of reading and following abstract reasoning, and who could be reached only through the senses.

Striving to establish a firm bond between the feudal lords and Divinity, art stressed the identification of noblemen with sacred figures. For example: the presentation of figures of noblemen and saints, especially in Romanesque art, was frontal, and they could never be painted working but only in idleness, characteristic of the powerful lord. Jesus was depicted as if he were a nobleman, and the nobleman as if he were Jesus. Unfortunately, Jesus was crucified and died after intense physical suffering, and here the identification no longer interested the nobility. Even in scenes of the most intense suffering, therefore, Jesus, Saint Sebastian, and other martyrs showed no sign of pain in their faces; on the contrary, they contemplated heaven with a strange bliss. The pictures in which Jesus appears crucified give the impression that he is barely leaning on a small pedestal and from there contemplates the happiness caused by the prospect of soon returning to the tender company of his Celestial Father.

It is not by chance that the principal theme of Romanesque painting was the Last Judgement. This theme is indeed the most apt to intimidate poor mortals, showing them terrible punishments and eternal spiritual pleasures, for their choice. It serves, besides, to remind the faithful that their earthly sufferings are merely a substantial accumulation of good deeds which will be credited to them in the ledger of Saint Peter, who closes the individual account of each one of us, at the moment of our death, and checks our credits and debits. This account book is a Renaissance invention which even today works miracles, bringing happiness to those sufferers who have enough faith in Paradise.

Like painting, the theater also tended toward the abstract in form and toward indoctrination in content. It is often said that the medieval theater was non-Aristotelian. We believe that this statement is based on the least important aspect of the *Poetics*, that is, on the unfortunately famous law of the three unities. This law has no validity as such, and not even the Greek tragedians obeyed the law rigorously. It is no more than a simple suggestion, given in an almost casual and incomplete form. Aristotle's *Poetics* is, above all, a perfect device for the exemplary social functioning of the theater. It is an efficient tool for the correction of men capable of modifying society. The *Poetics* must be dealt with in the light of this social aspect, for here alone lies its fundamental importance.

In tragedy, what was important for Aristotle was its cathartic function, its function as a "purifier" of the citizen. All his theories combine to form an harmonic whole which demonstrates the correct manner of purging the audience of all ideas or tendencies capable of modifying society. In this sense, the medieval theater was Aristotelian, though it did not utilize the same formal resources suggested by the Greek theoretician.

The typically feudal characters were not human beings, but rather abstractions of moral, religious values; they did not exist in the real, concrete world. The most typical were called Lust, Sin, Virtue, Angel, Devil, etc. They were not character-subjects of the dramatic action, but simply objects acting as spokesmen for the values they symbolized. The Devil, for example, had no free initiative; he merely fulfilled his task of tempting mankind, mouthing the phrases that that abstraction would necessarily use on such occasions. Likewise, the Angel, Lust, and all the other characters who symbolized good and evil, right and wrong, the just and unjust, obviously acted according to the perspective of the nobility and the clergy who patronized that art. The feudal plays were always of a moralizing and exemplary nature: the good were rewarded and the bad were punished.

They could be divided roughly in two groups: plays of sin and plays of virtue.

Among the plays of virtue, we can recall *The Representation and Commemoration of Abraham and Isaac, his Son,* by Belcari, almost a contemporary of Machiavelli. The play tells the story of that faithful servant of God, always ready to obey, even when the order from above is incomprehensible and unjust. (In the same way that every vassal had to obey his master, without questioning the justice of his commands.) Abraham, a good vassal, was always ready to obey the orders received from Heaven. The play narrates his fulfillment of duty, and then the intervention *a la* Hitchcock of an angel who appears on stage at the exact moment in which Abraham is bringing the sword down upon the tender, innocent neck of his son, as his sacred duty requires. The angel rejoices with father and son, praising the servile behavior of both and revealing the great reward they will receive for having obeyed so blindly the will of God, the Supreme Sovereign; as a reward, God offers Abraham the key to the door of his enemies. One may suppose that the enemies were not such good vassals as Abraham.

Among the plays of sin, one outstanding example, also a rather late work, was written by an anonymous English author: *Everyman.* It tells the story of Everyman at the time of his death and indicates the correct procedure for gaining absolution at that critical time, no matter how great the sins one may have committed. Absolution is won by repenting, doing an arduous penance, and, of course, by the providential appearance of an angel bearing the pardon and the moral of the story. Although lately angels have not often been seen here on earth, this play continues to be performed with considerable success and still evokes certain fears.

It is not so strange, after all, that the two examples cited — perhaps the most typical of feudal dramaturgy — were written when the bourgeoisie was already rather well developed and strong: the content becomes clear as social contradictions become sharper. Nor is it strange that the most typically bourgeois theater is being written today — when the bourgeoisie has reached the beginning of its end.

Plays that are too narrowly directed toward a single purpose run the risk of contradicting a fundamental principle of theater, which is conflict, contradiction, or some type of clash or combat. How did the medieval theater solve this problem? By putting the adversaries on stage, but showing them in such a way and manipulating the plot so that the denouement could be determined beforehand. In other words, by adopting a narrative style and placing the action in the past, thus avoiding the dramaticity and the direct, contemporaneous presentation of the characters in conflict. Karl Vossler observes curiously that he does not know of a single medieval drama in which the Devil is conceived and presented as a worthy adversary of God: he is fundamentally the vanquished, subordinated character.[4] His role is often secondary and many times comic. Even nowadays it is customary to have the Devil speak a foreign tongue, a device designed to place him in a ridiculous light, which at the same time weakens one of the parties to the conflict.

Unfortunately for the feudal nobility, nothing is eternal in this world, including the social and political systems which appear, develop, and give way to others that will have a similar fate. And with the rising bourgeoisie there arose a new type of art, a new poetics which began to give expression to new knowledge, acquired and transmitted according to a new perspective. Machiavelli is one of the witnesses of those social and artistic transformations. Machiavelli initiates the poetics of *virtù*.

The Bourgeois Concretion

With the development of commerce, starting as early as the eleventh century, life started moving from the country to the newly founded cities, where warehouses were built and banks were established, where commercial accounting was organized and trade was centralized. The slow pace of the Middle Ages was replaced by the fast pace of the Renaissance. This rapidity was due to the fact that each person started to build for himself rather than for the glory of the eternal God, who, eternal as He was, did not seem to be in a hurry to receive the proofs of love given by his fearful worshipers, as Alfred von Martin writes in his *Sociology of the Renaissance*. In the Middle Ages the construction of a church or a castle could take centuries, since it was built for the community and for God. Beginning with the Renaissance, construction came to be for mortal men themselves, and no one could wait indefinitely.[5]

The methodic organization of life, of all human activities, became one of the principal values contributed by the rising bourgeoisie. To spend less than one makes, to economize strength and money, to economically manage the body as well as the mind, to be a hard worker in contrast to the idleness of the medieval nobility: those became the means by which each enterprising individual could rise socially and prosper.[6] The rising bourgeoisie encouraged the development of science because it was necessary for its objective of promoting increased production, which would bring greater profits and an accumulation of capital. It was as necessary to discover new routes to the Indies as it was to discover new techniques of production and new machines that would increase the yield of the labor rented by the bourgeois.

Even war began to be conducted in a much more technical manner than before, mainly because of the new firearms, now made more efficient and used more freely. The ideals of knighthood were destined necessarily to disappear, for dozens of brave Cids Campeadores could be eliminated with the shot of a single cannon, fired by the most fainthearted and cowardly soldier.

In the new society organized on accounting principles, writes von Martin, the individual ability and value of each man became more important than the social estate in which they were born, and even God himself came to be the supreme judge of financial transactions, the invisible organizer of this world, which was itself considered to be a great commercial enterprise.[7] Man's relations with God were conceived in terms of debits and credits, a practice which even today corresponds to the Catholic view of good deeds. Charity is the contractual way of assuring oneself of divine help. Goodness gave place to charity.

This new proprietor-God, the bourgeois God, demanded an urgent religious reformulation, which was not long in coming, through the formula of Protestantism. Luther said that prosperity was nothing more than the reward given by God for the good conduct of business affairs, for the good management of material goods. And for Calvin there was no surer way to lay claim as a chosen one of God than to become rich here on earth. If God should look with disfavor upon a certain individual, He would not allow him to become rich. If he did become rich, that meant that God was on his side. Accumulated capital thus came to be a sign of divine grace. The poor, those who worked with their hands, the workers and peasants, were merely a legion of the non-elect, who could not become rich because God was against them, or at least did not help them. In Machiavelli's comedy the *Mandragola*, Friar Timoteo utilized the Bible in a typically Renaissance manner, showing that the Scriptures had lost their normative function in the behavior of men, to become instead a holy repository of texts, deeds, and versicles which, interpreted out of context, could justify *a posteriori* any attitude, thought, or act — whether of clergy or laymen — no matter how base it might be. And when the play was presented for the first time, Pope Leo X not only approved it, but was extremely pleased that Machiavelli, with extraordinary accuracy, had given artistic expression to the new religious mentality and the new principles of the Church.

In spite of all those social changes, the bourgeois suffered a great disadvantage in comparison to the feudal lord: while the latter could assert that his power emanated from what was in effect a contract made back in immemorial times — in which God Himself had given him (the feudal lord) the right to possess the land, together with the right of being God's representative on earth — the bourgeois could allege nothing in his own defense, unless it were his enterprising spirit, his own individual value and ability.

His birth did not give him special rights; if any were his, it was because he had won them with money, free initiative, work, and the cold, rational ability to give method to life. Bourgeois power, therefore, rested on the individual value of man living in the concrete circumstances of the real world. The bourgeois owed nothing to his fate or his good fortune, but only to his own *virtù*. With his *virtù* he had surmounted all the obstacles which were placed before him by birth, the laws of the feudal system, tradition, religion. His *virtù* was the first law.

But this able bourgeois who denied all traditions and disowned the past, what other guidelines for behavior could he choose if not those of reality itself? Right and wrong, good and bad — these can be known only in relation to practice. Nor could any law or tradition, but only the material and concrete world, provide him with the sure ways to attain power. Praxis was the second law of the bourgeoisie.

Virtù and praxis were and are the two touchstones of the bourgeoisie, its two principal characteristics. Obviously one cannot conclude from this that only he who was not a nobleman could possess *virtù* or trust in praxis, and much less that every bourgeois had necessarily to possess those qualities, under penalty of ceasing to be a bourgeois. Machiavelli himself criticized the bourgeoisie of his time, accusing it of placing too much value on tradition, of dreaming excessively of the romantic rules of the feudal nobility, thereby weakening itself and delaying the consolidation of its positions and the creation of its own values. This new society had to produce inevitably a new type of art, radically different. The new class could not, by any means, utilize the existing artistic abstractions, but on the contrary was compelled to turn toward concrete reality in its search for new forms of art. It could not tolerate characters with the old values inherited from feudalism. On stage and in paintings and sculptures, it needed to create live men, of flesh and blood, especially the "virtuous" man.

In painting, one need only leaf through any book on the history of art to become aware of what took place. The canvases began to show individuals surrounded by true landscapes. Even in the Gothic style, the faces had already begun to be individualized. Bourgeois art was, in all respects, a popular art; it not only parted with the traditional relations with the Church, but also started to depict familiar figures.

One of the most remarkable developments of bourgeois art was the appearance of the naked figure. . . . Not only clerical but also aristocratic culture were opposed to the representation of the nude. "Nakedness, like death, is democratic" (Jul. Lange). The many pictures of the Dance of Death, products of the late and increasingly bourgeois Middle Ages, proclaim the equality of all in the face of death. But when the bourgeoisie ceased to regard itself as suppressed, when it became conscious of its own rise to power, it could through its artists place Man naked and himself in the center of life.[8]

In theater the abstract figure of the Devil, for example, disappeared and individualized devils appeared — Lady Macbeth, Iago, Cassius, Richard III, and others of lesser power. They were not merely the "principle of evil" or "diabolic angels," or some equivalent, but live men who freely opted for the paths considered to be evil.

They were "virtuous" men, in the Machiavellian sense, who took advantage of all their potentials, trying to eliminate every trace of emotion, living in a purely intellectual and calculating world. The intellect absolutely lacks moral character. It is neutral, like money.[9]

It is no surprise to find that one of the most typically Shakespearian themes is that of the seizing of power by someone who has no legal right to do so. Neither did the bourgeoisie have the "right" to seize power, but it did it nevertheless. Shakespeare told the history of the bourgeoisie in the form of fable. His situation was dichotomous: although his sympathy, as playwright and man, was decidedly with Richard III (the virtuous man dies, the symbolic representative of the rising class, the man who acts with confidence in his own *virtù*, defeating tradition and the established and consecrated social order), Shakespeare must have been inclined, consciously or not, toward the nobility that patronized him and which, after all, still retained political power. Richard is unquestionably the hero even though he ends up being defeated in the fifth act. It was always in the fifth act that such things occurred, and they did not always occur convincingly: the manner in which Macbeth is defeated by the representatives of legality, Malcolm and Macduff — one the legitimate heir, evasive and cowardly, and the other his faithful servant and vassal — is open to censure, at least from the dramatic point of view. Hauser throws light on that dichotomy when he recalls that Queen Elizabeth was one of the greatest debtors of the English banks, which shows that the nobility itself was dichotomous.[10] Shakespeare expressed the new bourgeois values which were then arising, even if legality and feudalism are the apparent victors at the end of his plays.

The entire body of Shakespeare's dramatic works serves as documentary evidence of the coming of the individualized man in the theater. His central characters are always analyzed multidimensionally. It would be difficult to find in the dramaturgy of any other country or period, a character comparable to Hamlet; he is analyzed extensively in all dimensions: in his love relationship with Ophelia, his friendship with Horatio, his political relationship with King Claudius and Fortinbras, in his metaphysical and psychological dimensions, etc. Shakespeare was the first dramatist to proclaim man in all his plenitude, as no other dramatist had done before, without excluding even Euripides. Hamlet is not abstract doubt, but a man who, facing some very precise circumstances, doubts. Othello is not jealousy in itself, but simply a man capable of killing the woman he loves because he believes her to be unfaithful. Romeo is not *love*, but a boy that falls in love with a certain girl named Juliet, who has obstinate parents and a determined maid, and he suffers the fatal consequences of his love adventures in beds and graves.

What happened to the character in theater? He simply ceased to be an object and became a subject of the dramatic action. The character was converted into a bourgeois conception.

Being the first dramatist of *virtù* and praxis, Shakespeare is
— in this, and only this, sense — the first bourgeois dramatist. He
was the first who knew how to depict to the fullest extent, the
fundamental characteristics of the new class. Before him, including during the Middle Ages, there were plays and authors that
made attempts in the same direction: Hans Sachs in Germany,
Ruzzante in Italy (not to mention Machiavelli), *La Farce de
Maître Pierre Pathelin* in France, etc.

It is necessary to emphasize that — other than in exceptional
cases such as Antonio, the merchant of Venice — Shakespeare
did not portray heroes who were avowedly bourgeois. Richard III
is also the Duke of Gloucester. The bourgeois nature of the works
of Shakespeare is not to be found in their externals at all, but only
in the presentation and creation of characters endowed with *virtù*
and confident in praxis. In the formal aspects, his theater manifests what can be considered feudal residues: the common people
speak in prose and the noblemen in verse, for example.

One criticism, the most serious that can be made to these
statements, is that the bourgeoisie — because of its own condition
as alienator of man — would not be the class most likely to give
rise to human multidimensionality.

We believe that this would be true if a sudden, brusque leap
were made between two social systems following in succession, if
one ceased to exist in the exact moment in which the other appeared. That is, if the bourgeoisie created its own superstructure
of values in the very moment in which the first bourgeois rented
the labor-power of the first worker and from him obtained the first
surplus value. Since this does not happen, let us take a closer
look.

Actually, Shakespeare did not show the multidimensionality
of all men, all the characters, or the human species in general, but
only of some men who possessed certain exceptional qualities,
that is, those endowed with *virtù*. The exceptionality of these men
was strongly marked in two opposite directions: against the impo-
tent and ruined nobility, and against the people in general, the
amorphous mass. In the first case it is enough to recall some
fundamental conflicts revolving around the central characters.
What are those who oppose Macbeth if not mediocre people?
Duncan and Malcolm have no individual value that merits distinction. Richard III confronts a whole court of decadent noblemen,

beginning with the sickly Edward IV; they are a group of gossips, inconstant and weak. And regarding the rottenness of Denmark, it is unnecessary to add anything to the words of the prince himself.

On the other hand, the people either remain in the background or are easily fooled and passively accept the change of masters (*Machiavelli:* "The people easily accept the change of masters because they believe, in vain, that their lot is thereby going to improve.") The people are manipulated by the will of the "virtuous" men. Remember the scene in which Brutus and later Marcus Antonius inflame the people, swaying them first one way and then another. The people are a shapeless and malleable mass. Where were the people when Richard and Macbeth were committing their crimes, or when Lear divided his kingdom? These are questions which do not interest Shakespeare.

The bourgeoisie asserted one type of exceptional condition as opposed to another: the extraordinary individual in contrast to those privileged by estate. While its principal opposition was to the feudal nobility, the bourgeoisie directed its energies toward the exaltation of individual man — the same man who was later submitted to severe reduction, by that same bourgeoisie, when its principal opponent came to be the proletariat. But it waited for the right moment to take on this new opponent and only started to perform this role when it definitively assumed political power; when, as Marx said, the words of the slogan *Liberté, Egalité, Fraternité!* were replaced by others which translated better their true meaning: Infantry, Cavalry, Artillery! Only then did the bourgeoisie begin to reduce the man it had exalted.

Machiavelli and *Mandragola*

Mandragola is a play typical of the transition between the feudal
and the bourgeois theater, and its characters contain, in equal
measure, abstraction as well as concretion. They are not yet
human beings completely individualized and multidimensional,
but they are no longer mere symbols and signs. They synthesize
individual characteristics and abstract ideas, in a perfect balance.

In the prologue, Machiavelli apologizes for having written a
theatrical work — a light genre, lacking in austerity. He seems to
believe that he must simply entertain the spectators, making them
think as little as possible and delighting them with a story of love
and gallantry. For this he utilizes a humorous case of adultery
while continuing to think about the serious, grave matters that
concern him.

Machiavelli believes that the taking of power (or conquering
the woman one loves) can only be effected through cold, calculating reason, free of any preoccupations of a moral nature and
entirely directed toward the feasibility and efficacy of the scheme
to be adopted and developed. This is the main idea of the play and
divides the characters roughly into two groups: the "virtuous"
and the "nonvirtuous," that is, those who believe in, and are
guided by, that premise, and those who do not believe in it.

Ligurio is the play's central character, the pivotal character
and the most "virtuous." He is a metamorphosis of the Devil,
who in him begins to acquire free initiative. Ligurio is not the

conventional parasite, of long tradition in the history of the theater. He is a man endowed with great *virtù* who freely chose to be a parasite, as he could have chosen to be a monk or priest. It matters little that the author utilized an existing theatrical figure: what matters is the figure's new content. Ligurio only believes in his own intelligence, in his ability to solve, through the intellect, all the problems that may arise. He never trusts in chance, good luck, or fate, as does Callimaco; he has faith only in the schemes he thinks out beforehand and then carries out methodically. At no time does any thought or concern of a moral nature cross his mind except when he meditates on the wickedness of men. He meditates without lamenting the fact, only with an acute sense of the practical and utilitarian. He meditates coldly, as Machiavelli himself would do, about the good and the bad use that can be made of cruelty, without attributing to cruelty in itself any moral value. In this respect there is a certain kinship between Machiavelli and Brecht. The latter is also capable of writing that sometimes it is necessary "to lie or to tell the truth, to be honest or dishonest, cruel or compassionate, charitable or a thief." Praxis must be the only determining factor in the behavior of man. Ligurio has no particular personal style of behavior. He is a chameleon. Given the profession he has chosen, he knows that he must be accommodating, varying his personality in accordance with each particular situation and each objective to be obtained. Talking to the doctor, he is refined, trying in this way to make Messer feel himself to be a connoisseur of men and of the feminine beauties to be found in Florence. With Callimaco, he pretends to be his altruistic friend, ready to help him in his anguish. Devoutly he helps Friar Timoteo in his untiring search for God and better financial conditions. For a better understanding of Ligurio it would be advisable, at the very least, to read rapidly Dale Carnegie and other contemporary modern American authors who teach the art of succeeding in life.

Friar Timoteo, the opposite of Nicia, is also "virtuous," and very soon comes to understand Ligurio — with whom he becomes very close, to the advantage of both. The two carry out a plan from which they try to eliminate any interference of chance, and in which only the knowledge that both have of men, such as they really are, intervenes. Ligurio knows that men are bad because of their great attachment to money, the common denominator of moral values. In possession of this useful knowledge Ligurio knows that he will succeed in any enterprise, as long as he does not give any importance to such superfluous values as honor, dignity, loyalty, and other quaint medieval virtues. Everything can be translated into florins. Ligurio's scheme is neither malicious, immoral, nor perverse; it is merely astute and practical, the only one capable of realizing the incredible, almost impossible feat of seducing Madonna Lucrezia — honorable, devout, insensible to carnal pleasures (at least she prays enough to believe in all that), who is distant, modest, and before whose fidelity and rectitude even the servants feel an awesome fear. All is possible in this world as long as one takes the reality of men into account, without exalting them, without praising or criticizing them: only taking them as they truly are and profiting from that.

Friar Timoteo, for his part, is not a corrupt friar, but rather the symbol of a new religious mentality. Just as the Renaissance world in general becomes commercialized (and we should remember that even Fray Luis de León compares women to precious gems, not because of their spiritual values but because of the possibility they have of being hoarded), thus also our friar admits that the Church must take heed of its finances in order to survive. Timoteo thinks this way not in bad faith, but rather because he understands the nature of the new times and knows that one must either keep up with the times or fade away. He assimilates the new truths, accepts the new practices, adjusts to the new society. He keeps the saintly teachings of the Bible and the Church finances in the same book. Like Luther later on, Timoteo already believes that the sacred book can and should be interpreted with flexibility according to each specific and individual case. There should not exist a dogmatic interpretation which has, objectively, the same meaning and value for all. Each one of us must enter into direct contact with God and the Holy teachings, and in this subjective man-God relationship we will find more easily the happiness we need on earth as well as in Heaven. The Bible comes to serve merely as an aid for the friar, to explain and support his decisions. Thus the naive behavior of Lot's daughters serves to justify the adultery of Lucrezia. In all things one must consider the goal: Lucrezia's goal is to fill a vacancy in Paradise, and that is what counts. If to do so, she has to betray her husband, it matters little: her only concern is to be centered on the little soul that will be delivered to the world and to God. Moses would surely be surprised at this curious interpretation of his text! This amorality of Timoteo is questioned in a single monologue in which he manifests regrets, stating that bad companions can lead a good man to the gallows. We believe, however, that Timoteo does not really have a guilty conscience, nor a heavy heart, nor anything of the kind. We doubt that Timoteo feels repentant for the sins he may have committed; he is simply very sad for having been deceived by Ligurio. Both had agreed to a contract in which the friar would receive the sum of three hundred ducats. But that contract did not foresee the need of the disguise with which Messer Nicia fooled him once more; Timoteo laments the mockery of his good faith, as well as the fact that he has to pay more than was originally agreed upon. He would have been very happy if his share of florins had increased, even if the number of his sins had increased at the same time.

In this trajectory from Heaven to earth, all values become earthly. Even God Himself becomes humanized. For Timoteo, He ceases to be the distant God, reachable only through fervent prayers. Timoteo talks colloquially with God, though still assuming a subservient position, just as if God were the owner of a commercial firm in which Timoteo acts as manager. In his monologues the friar gives account to the Proprietor of his earthly affairs. Timoteo is a symbol of the Church which makes its triumphant entry into the mercantilist era. But in entering it does not scorn any of the elements of the traditional rituals, of the paternal affection which must characterize the members of the clergy as the means of facilitating the performance of their functions. The great theatrical impact of the friar is due precisely to this dichotomy: he speaks in the most spiritual tone possible in the moments in which he treats the most material financial affairs.

Thus Machiavelli produces a forceful demystifying effect, which retains much of the hyperbolic process of Aristophanes, or of his more recent disciples, Voltaire and Arapua. All these authors, each in his own medium, demystify the "eternal" truths. But they do not do it through the traditional process of denying them, but by making them untenable through an excess of affirmation — by making them absurd.

To the roll of "virtuous" characters still another remains to

be added: Sostrata, the mother of Lucrezia, who is a kind of retired woman of *virtù*. In her distant youth she was a respectable and dignified owner of a brothel. That, however, in no way detracts from her spotless character nor does it affect the good manners of the court. Especially now that she is a wealthy woman. Her trade differs hardly if at all from any other type of trade, and it even has some interesting advantages: the products marketed are the workers themselves, making it possible to obtain from them a stimulating increase of surplus value.

The notary Nicia is one of the most captivating characters in the entire history of theater. Having become wealthy with the development of urban life, he mourns at the prospect of dying without leaving an heir to whom he might bequeath his fortune, avariciously hidden. Like most bourgeois, he would prefer to have been born a prince or a count, or at least a baron. Since that unfortunately did not occur, he wants his behavior to resemble that of noblemen as much as possible. In his crucial moment in the second act, Nicia agrees to allow his wife to go to bed with a stranger, only because some noblemen — like the King of France and so many others among those aristocrats — had done so. It is an admirable scene. Nicia suffers terribly with the permitted adultery and at the same time feels happy with the prospect of gaining an heir, imitating the French nobility. He feels noble even though it hurts him. Faced with such ingenuousness, Liguria manipulates Nicia easily — using him nevertheless with some sympathy.

Lucrezia is the key figure in the dramatic change that takes place. Before meeting Callimaco, she conducted her life in such an exemplary manner that she could only be praised by Fray Luis de León *(The Perfect Wife)* or by Juan Luis Vives *(Instructions for the Christian Woman)*. She was the symbol desired by those two writers. She spent her time reading the lives of the purest, most chaste saints, avoiding even those who might have some pardoned sins. She took care of her husband's treasures, never daring to steal a look through the grill of the half-open window. Above all, Lucrezia prayed. And the more her body felt indefinable sensations, the more devout she became. Many women have lived like her and died feeling the anguish of an unfulfilled life. Lucrezia also believed that what she lacked was the sweet breath of angels, the tender caress of the inhabitants of Paradise. For her happiness to be complete, Lucrezia only needed to die. Or if not, she needed Callimaco; and he was not long in coming.

As idea, she represents, at the beginning of the play, the medieval abstraction of the honorable, pure woman. Her sweet transition corresponds to the appearance of the Renaissance woman, more attached to earthly things, with feet on the ground. She represents, as Machiavelli would say, the difference between "how one should live and how one actually lives." Even after the miraculous change has taken place, however, she continues to think of Heaven and does not abandon any of the old values: she simply begins to use them in the most prudent and pleasant manner. She accepts the new pleasures, enjoyed more by the flesh than by the spirit, and sees in them not sin, but obedience to divine will: "If this has happened to me, it can only be by God's determination, and I do not feel strong enough to refuse what Heaven wants me to accept."

The remaining characters, the widow and Siro, are of less significance. The widow serves almost exclusively as a means of revealing, in the first scene, the peculiar manner of thinking of the friar and his ability to translate everything into monetary terms. When she asks him if the Turks will invade Italy, Friar Timoteo answers without hesitation that it all depends on the prayers and masses that she may order to be said. The prayers are free, but the masses must be paid for, and paid well. The widow pays for masses so that the Turks will not invade Italy, pays for masses so that her unforgettable husband may pass from Purgatory into Paradise — pays, finally, in order to be forgiven for her peccadillos, caused by the fact that the flesh is weak and there is no strong spirit to dominate it.

As for Siro, he is a little more than the traditional servant who does everything for the comfort and well-being of his masters, caring for their interests and aiding in carrying out their plans. He is the least developed character in the play; from a technical viewpoint, his function is limited to what he says, helping Callimaco to tell the audience the antecedents of the story.

We believe that any staging of this play must follow a line of maximum clarity and sobriety of means. One must not forget that this text was written by Machiavelli and that Machiavelli had some important things to say. The use of a simple love story and of characters such as Nicia, Sostrata, Lucrezia, and the others is purely circumstantial, serving only to present in an amusing and

theatrical manner — in figurative form — the practical functioning of the "virtuous" man. In staging a play, the director's freedom decreases as the intellectual precision of the playwright increases. Thus the director needs to maintain clarity as he translates Machiavelli's ideas into the language of theater.

Mandragola is also one of the most successful examples of
popular dramaturgy. The conventional belief is that popular theater must be close to circus, whether as text or as performance.
This opinion is widespread and generally accepted. We disagree
absolutely, just as we would disagree with anyone who would
state that TV drama, given its peculiar emotional violence, is a
valid form of popular art. We believe, on the contrary, that the
most important characteristic of the theater which addresses itself
to the people must be its permanent clarity, its ability to reach the
spectator — appealing to his intelligence and sensitivity — without circumlocution or mystification. *Mandragola* relates to the
spectator in an intelligent manner, and when it succeeds in moving him, it does so through reason, through thought and never
through an empathic, abstractly emotional bond. And in this re-
sides its most significant popular quality.

Modern Reductions of *Virtù*

Perhaps the bourgeoisie in its initial impetus has taken the frontiers of theater too far. The type of man it created threatened to expand. Shakespearean drama itself, even if severely limited, could serve as a double-edged sword, opening up new paths that could lead in unknown, and possibly dangerous, directions. The bourgeoisie soon realized this fact, and as it assumed political power, it began the task of taking away from theater the same weapons that it — the bourgeoisie itself, and for its own benefit — had given to the theater. Machiavelli proposed the liberation of man from all moral values. Shakespeare followed those instructions to the letter, though he always repented in the fifth act and restored legality and morality. It was necessary for someone to come along who, without renouncing the freedom recently acquired by the dramatic character, could impose some limitations upon him, working out a formula that might preserve his formal freedom, though insuring that the dogmatic pre-established truth would prevail. That someone was Hegel.

Hegel asserted that the character is free, that is, that the inner movements of his soul must always be capable of being exteriorized, without hindrance. But to be free did not mean that the character could be capricious and do whatever he wished: freedom is the consciousness of ethical necessity. He must not, however, exercise his freedom with regard to the purely accidental or episodical, but only regarding situations and values common to all mankind or to nationality — eternal powers, moral truths such as love, filial love, patriotism, etc. . . . .

In this way, Hegel succeeds in making the character embody an ethical principle, and his freedom consists only in giving that principle a concrete form in the exterior world, in real life. Abstract moral values acquire concrete spokesmen, who are the characters. No longer, as in the feudal theater, is Goodness a character called just that, Goodness; now its name is John Doe or Bill Smith. Goodness and John Doe are one and the same, though different: one is the abstract value, the other its human concretion. Those characters, therefore, immanently embody an "eternal" value, a "moral" truth or its antithesis. If there is to be drama, conflict is necessary. Thus the characters who embody those values come into conflict with the characters who incorporate their antitheses. The dramatic action is the result of the peripeteia produced by those struggles.

The action, according to Hegel, must be conducted to a certain point where the balance can be restored. The drama must end in rest, in harmony. (We are still very far from Bertolt Brecht, whose view is exactly the opposite.) Nevertheless, how can this balance be reached, if not through the destruction of one of the antagonists who confront each other? It is necessary that the array of forces appearing as thesis-antithesis be taken to the state of synthesis, and in theater that can only be done in one of two ways: death of one of the irreconcilable characters (tragedy) or repentance (romantic or social drama, according to the Hegelian system).

However — and it is Hegel himself who says so — the drama, as any other art, is the "radiance of truth" shining through the sensory means which the artist utilizes. But how can the truth shine if the character who is carrier of the "eternal" truth is destroyed? It is necessary that error be punished. The character who embodies falsehood must die or repent. Hegel could accept, at the most, the death of the concrete hero, the real man, if through that catastrophe the truth he carried would shine with greater brilliance. And this often occurred in Romanticism.

Romanticism re-edited the feudal theme of the Last Judg-bourgeois world, even if only against its exterior, incidental aspects. It apparently struggled against the bourgeois values. But what did it propose in exchange? Hegel answers: Love, Honor,

Loyalty. That is, the values of the code of chivalry, a poorly disguised return to medieval abstractions, now in a theater formulated with greater theoretic precision and greater complexity. Romanticism re-edited the feudal theme of the Last Judgment — the post-terrestrial reward. How else are we to interpret the final words of Doña Sol in *Hernani* when, at the moment of death, she talks of the marvelous flight which the two lovers will take, upon dying, in search of a better world. True life and true happiness are impossible. It is as if they said: "This world is too repugnant and abject. Here only the bourgeois, with their petty material interests, can be happy. Let's leave the sordid bourgeois, their sordid happiness, and their sordid money which only buys sordid pleasures. We shall be eternally blessed. Let's commit suicide!" No bourgeois would feel seriously offended by such propositions.

Romanticism could be considered merely as a swan song of the feudal nobility, if it were not also of a markedly mystifying and alienating character. Arnold Hauser analyzes the true meaning of the *Roman d'un jeune homme pauvre*, showing that Octave Feuillet tries to inculcate the reader with the idea that a man, though poor and miserable, can and should possess true aristocratic dignity, which is essentially spiritual. The material conditions of each person's life matter very little: values are the same for all men.[11]

It was an attempt to solve in the field of the spirit the problems facing men in society. Everyone, without distinction, could aspire to spiritual perfection, even if he were poor like Jean Valjean, deformed like Rigoletto, or a pariah like Hernani. Men, even though hungry, must preserve that marvelous thing called spiritual freedom. The writers who give the most beautiful expression to that belief are undoubtedly Victor Hugo and Hegel. This was the first serious reduction imposed upon man in the theater: he came to be weighed in relation to eternal, immutable values.

Realism, highly praised by Marx (but for other reasons) represented the second great reduction: man became the direct product of his environment. It is true that in the hands of its first practitioners realism did not reach the dimensions of sterility which it took on later. Obviously, Marx could not even imagine what Sidney Kingsley, Tennessee Williams and others of our days would do. And Marx was referring mainly to realism in the novel, which produced extensive sociological studies of bourgeois life.

The main realist limitation in the theater consists in its presenting a reality which is supposedly already known. From the naturalistic point of view, the work of art will be as good as its success in reproducing reality. Antoine[12] took this premise to its logical extreme by giving up the reproduction of reality and conveying reality itself to the stage: in one of his productions he used real meat in a scene which depicted a butcher shop.

Zola, expounding his famous theory that the theater must show a "slice of life," even wrote that the playwright must not take sides, displaying life exactly as it is, without even being selective. The vulnerability of this argument is so obvious that it is unnecessary to demonstrate that the very choice of theme, story, and characters already implies a position taken by the author. Zola's statement is important, however, insofar as it points to the dead end at which naturalistic objectivity arrived: photographic reality. Beyond that point it was not possible, objectively, to continue. But there was a different way, in the opposite direction — toward increasing subjectivity. After Shakespeare, man was never shown multidimensionally on the stage. When the objective movement ended, a series of subjective styles ensued: impressionism, expressionism, surrealism. All of them tending to restore a freedom that was, nevertheless, merely subjective. Abstract emotions — fear, terror, anguish — appeared. All in the mind of the character who projected outwardly his phantasmagoric world.

Even realism sought out man's inner ways, delving into psychology, but even there it fell short. It reduced man to psychoalgebraic equations. In order to realize what happened, it is enough to remember some of the latest productions of Williams and other authors of his school. The recipe varies very little: by bringing together a father who has abandoned the mother after the birth of the first child and a mother who is an alcoholic, we will no doubt obtain a character whose defect is bound to be some type of generalized sadomasochism. If the mother is unfaithful — the arithmetic does not fail — the son will be a delicate sexual invert.

From that point on, the evolution could logically move in

only one direction, and Tennessee Williams — an author gifted with a great talent — could not fail to follow it: the literal chewing up of the protagonist's sexual organs. It is not without a certain originality. . . . To go farther would be to enter a convent, and we believe that sooner or later Williams will take that step, too. The theater has also tried to follow the paths of mysticism: the search for God as an escape from material problems. Eugene O'Neill stated more than once that his interest was not in the relations between men but only in the relations of man with God.

In the absence of God, O'Neill directs his interest toward the mysterious and supernatural forces that surround us and which we cannot explain. Explicable phenomena do not seem to interest him. His eyes are "beyond the horizon" in search of tragic destinies, or expectant as he lies in wait for new gods. As long as they do not come, O'Neill goes on fabricating his own for home use. Isn't that what happens in *Dynamo*? The playwright almost projects himself into the terrain of science fiction. In the same way that he discovered the God Dynamo, he would — if he were still alive — already have discovered the God Sputnik, the God Magnetic Belt, and other inhabitants of the modern and scientific Olympus.

The bourgeoisie, perhaps aided by Hollywood statistics, recently discovered the enormous persuasive power of the theater and related arts. Having referred to Hollywood, we would like to give an example: in the film *It Happened One Night*, in a certain scene the actor Clark Gable takes off his shirt and reveals that he does not wear an undershirt. It was enough to bring several manufacturers of this article to bankruptcy as they lost those customers who were members of the various Clark Gable fan clubs and anxious to imitate their idol. The theater influences the spectators not only with respect to clothing but also in the spiritual values that can be inculcated in them through example. Thus a new "exemplary" type of play or film came into existence, which tries to reinforce some of the values revered by capitalist society, such as the art and ability to achieve success in life, through free enterprise. They are biographic plays and films that show the awesome career of certain citizens who climbed the ladder of fame and fortune, starting from the humblest circumstances of life. "If J. P. Morgan accumulated such a tremendous fortune, yachts, mansions, etc., why can't you do the same? Of course you can do it, too. You are obliged only to obey the rules of the game." That is, the capitalist game.

Marx once said that all historical events occur twice: the first time as tragedy, the second as comedy. This is what happened with the work of Machiavelli. His writings had a meaning of the utmost gravity. And today his American disciples, inspirers of that exemplary line of the theater and movies — Dale Carnegie and others — cannot avoid the comical element inevitably involved in their advice, expressed in books of the type of *How to Make Your Wife Keep On Loving You Tenderly, Even After She's Got a Lover Who's a Much Better Guy Than You Are*. If the reader would forgive the absurdity of the comparison, we would say that both Machiavelli and Dale Carnegie preach the slogan, "where there's a will there's a way" — the former with all the seriousness of a class in the process of imposing itself; the second as a present-day Yankee.

The most recent and severe reduction of man, however, is the one being effected by the antitheater of Eugène Ionesco, who tries to take away from man even his powers of communication. Man becomes incommunicable, not in the sense that he cannot express his innermost emotions or the nuances of his thought, but literally incommunicable — to the extent that all words can be translated into only one: "chat" *(Jack, or the Submission)*. All concepts equal "chat." Ionesco presents this absurdity with great humor, and we — bourgeois and petty bourgeois — respond with laughter. But to the workers awaiting an announcement from management in relation to an increase in wage levels, it would not seem so amusing to be given a speech such as the one which closes the play *The Chairs*, delivered by a mute messenger. Or to be told that "wage increase" is "chat," "poverty" is "chat," "hunger" is "chat," everything is "chat."

In making these analytical remarks and raising objections we do not mean to suggest that the authors are unimportant. On the contrary, we believe that they are extremely significant, insofar as they indeed testify to the final phase of the bourgeois society and theater. They bring to an end the trajectory of that theater in which the multidimensional man is repeatedly subjected to reductions that transform him entirely into new abstractions of a psychological, moral, or metaphysical nature. In this sense Ionesco overshadows the achievements of all his fellow playwrights in the enormous task of dehumanizing man. It was he who created the last bourgeois character, Bérenger, around whom all the characters gradually change into rhinoceroses, that is, into abstractions. What could become of the last representative of the human species — the last and only, when all the rest have disappeared — if he is not transformed precisely into the abstraction of the human species? Bérenger is merely the negation of the rhinoceros, and therefore he himself is an alienated non-rhinoceros. He is devoid of any content other than that of simple negation.

This has been the path of development followed by the theater since the appearance of the modern bourgeoisie. In opposition to that theater, another must rise: one determined by a new class and which will dissent not only stylistically but in a much more radical manner. This new theater, dialectically materialist, will necessarily be also a theater of abstractions, at least in its initial phase. Not only superstructural abstractions, but also infrastructural. Its characters will reveal, in some plays of Brecht, their condition of mere objects, objects of determined social functions which, by coming into contradiction, develop a system of forces that directs the movement of dramatic action.

It is a theater that has just been born, and which, though breaking with all the traditional forms, still suffers from an insufficiently formulated theoretical basis. Only out of constant practice will the new theory arise.

Notes for Chapter 2

[1] Arnold Hauser, *The Social History of Art*, trans. Stanley Godman, 4 vols. (New York: Vintage Books, Inc., 1957), 1:83, 85, 87.

[2] Hauser, 1:180-81.

[3] Hauser, 1:181-82.

[4] *Formas literarias en los pueblos románicos* (Buenos Aires: Espasa-Calpe, 1944), p. 22.

[5] Alfred von Martin, *Sociology of the Renaissance* (New York: Oxford University Press, 1944), p. 16.

[6] Von Martin, p. 17.

[7] Von Martin, pp. 17-19.

[8] Von Martin, pp. 26-27.

[9] Von Martin, pp. 37-38.

[10] Hauser, 2:149-50.

[11] Hauser, 4:89.

[12] A famous French theatrical director.

Hegel and Brecht:
The Character
as Subject or
the Character
as Object?

The "Epic" Concept

The greatest obstacle to comprehension of the extraordinary changes produced in the theater by the contribution of Marxism lies in a misunderstanding of the way in which certain terms are used. Precisely because those gigantic transformations were not immediately perceived, the new theories were explained with the old vocabulary: to designate new realities, old words were utilized. An attempt was made to use new connotations for words already worn out, and exhausted by their old denotations.

Let us take an example: what is the meaning of the word *epic*? In the beginning, Bertolt Brecht applied that old word to his theater. Aristotle does not speak of epic *theater*, but only of epic poetry, tragedy, and comedy. The differences that he establishes between epic poetry and tragedy refer to the verse (for him, necessarily present in the two forms), the duration of the action, and, finally — what is more important — to the fact that epic poetry is, as he sees it, formally "narrative," contrary to what happens in tragedy. While in the latter, action takes place in the present, in the former the action happened in the past and is now being recalled. Aristotle adds that all the elements of epic poetry are found in the tragedy, but not all the elements of tragedy are present in epic poetry. Basically, both "imitate" the actions of characters of a "superior type."

Erwin Piscator, a contemporary of Brecht, has in turn a completely different concept of the meaning of *epic*, or rather, he makes a type of theater completely different from what Aristotle understands by epic poetry and yet to that type of theater he applies the same name. For the first time in a theatrical spectacle, Piscator used motion pictures, slides, graphics, in short, all the mechanisms or resources that can help to explain the reality present in the text of a work. This absolute freedom of form, with the inclusion of any element until then unusual, was called by Piscator "epic" form. This immense formal richness broke the conventional *empathic* tie and produced an effect of *distance* — an effect that was later carried farther by Brecht, as we will soon see. When he staged Sartre's *The Flies* in New York — wanting to be sure that no spectator would fail to understand that Sartre was speaking about his own country, occupied by the Nazi German armed forces — Piscator ordered the exhibition, before the play, of a film about the war, the occupation, torture, and other evils of capitalism. Piscator did not want anyone to think that the play dealt with the Greeks, who were in this instance simply elements of a fable used to tell about things which were contemporary and pertinent.

Nowadays the word *epic* is fashionably applied in only one sense: in reference to some films about the mass murders of American Indians by government troops, or films about the expansionist war of the United States against Mexico — in short, films made in the "open air." This is the most frequent conception of the word: a film with many characters, many horses, gunfire, combat, and occasionally some love scenes, in the midst of deaths, blood, rape, and violence, in a package appropriate for an audience of eight years or older.

In all these usages the word *epic* has to do with that which is broad, exterior, long-term, objective, etc. As Brecht uses the term, it carries these meanings also, as well as some others.

Brecht uses the expression epic theater mainly in contraposition to Hegel's definition of epic poetry. In reality, Brecht's whole poetics is basically an answer and a counterproposal to the idealist poetics of Hegel.

In order to understand the meaning of *epic* for Hegel, it is necessary to recall initially that within his system of the arts, Hegel attributed fundamental importance to the greater or lesser degree in which "the spirit is liberated from matter." Let us explain it better by saying that art, for Hegel, was the shining of truth through matter. In accordance with this conception, he divided the arts into symbolic, classic, and romantic. In the first, matter predominates and the spirit is hardly visible. Architecture, for example, belongs to this category. In the second type, the spirit is a little more liberated from matter and achieves balance. It is the case of sculpture: the face of a man, his physiognomy, his expression, his thought, his pain, manage to pass through the marble. Finally, the arts called romantic are those in which the spirit is able to liberate itself completely from matter. This is the case with poetry. The matter of poetry is the words, not cement or marble. For this reason the spirit in poetry is able to reach refinements which are impossible in architecture, where the material substances of stone and earth heavily predominate.[1]

Types of Poetry in Hegel

For Hegel, epic poetry presents "a complete world, whose ideal or essential content must be spread before us under the external guise of human actions, events, and other manifestations of soul-life. . . "[2] For him all that happens arises from spiritual powers — sometimes divine, sometimes human — and from the exterior obstacles which react, retarding their movement. That is, the spirit of a god or of a man initiates an action which encounters difficulties in the exterior world: epic poetry narrates those encounters and those conflicts from the point of view of their occurrence in the exterior world and not in the spirit which originated them. The action acquires "the form of objective . . . , becomes an *event*, in which the facts in question disclose themselves in free independence, and the poet retires into the background." It is the deeds that are important and not the subjectivity of the poet who narrates them, or of the characters who perform them. The mission of epic poetry consists in remembering such events, "and by so doing it represents the *objective* fact itself in its objectivity."[3]

In telling how this or that battle developed, the epic poet must describe the battle with the maximum of objective details possible, without concerning himself with his particular manner of feeling the facts. A horse must be described as a horse, objectively, and not through the subjective images which might occur to one upon seeing a horse.

Lyric poetry is exactly opposite to epic poetry. "Its content is that within ourselves, the ideal world, the contemplative or emotional life of soul, which instead of following up actions, remains at home with itself in its own ideal realm, and, consequently, is able to accept *self-expression* as its unique and indeed final end."[4]

What is important in lyric poetry is not the horse it itself, but the emotions which the horse may arouse in the poet; it is not the concrete facts of a battle, but the resources of the poet's sensibility which are moved by the sound of the swords. Lyric poetry is completely subjective, personal.

Finally, dramatic poetry, in Hegel's view, combines the principle of objectivity (epic) with that of subjectivity (lyric): "In this we not only discover an *objective* exposition, but also can trace its source in the ideal life of particular people; what is objective here is therefore portrayed as appertinent to the conscious life of individuals."[5] The action is presented not as it is in the epic, as something already past, but rather as something that happens in the very moment in which we witness it. In epic poetry the action and the characters belong to a time that is different from that of the spectators; in dramatic poetry the spectators are transported to the time and the place where the action occurs — that is, they are in the same time and space as the characters, and hence are able to experience empathy, the present, living emotional rapport. Epic poetry "recalls"; dramatic poetry "relives."

Thus we see that in dramatic poetry subjectivity and objectivity co-exist, but it is important to note that, for Hegel, the former precedes the latter: the soul is the subject that determines all external action. Likewise, Aristotle held that the passions transformed into habits were the motive forces of action. In these two philosophers, the drama shows the external collision of forces originating internally — the *objective* conflict of *subjective* forces. For Brecht, as we shall see, everything is reversed.

Characteristics of Dramatic Poetry,
Still According to Hegel

Hegel thinks that we have the need to see human acts and relationships presented before us alive and direct. But, he adds,
"dramatic action . . . is not confined to the simple and undis-
turbed execution of a definite purpose, but depends throughout
on conditions of collision, human passion and characters, and
leads therefore to actions and reactions, which in their turn call
for some further resolution of conflict and disruption." It offers
the continually moving spectacle of struggle between living
characters who pursue opposite desires in the midst of situations
full of obstacles and dangers.[6]

Above all, Hegel insists on a fundamental point which will
mark a radical difference between his view and that of the Marxist
poetics of Brecht: "the event [writes Hegel] does not appear to
proceed from external conditions, but rather from personal volition and character. . . ."[7]

The denouement arises out of the dramatic conflict; it is, like
the action itself, both subjective and objective. It is the repose
that comes after the tumult of human passions and actions.[8] In
order for this to occur, the characters must necessarily be "free";
that is, it is necessary for the internal movements of their spirit to
be freely exteriorized without limitations or restraints. In short,
the character is the absolute *subject* of his actions.

Freedom of the Character-Subject

In order that the character may be truly free, no limitations are to be placed on his action, except those that are imposed by the will of another character, equally free. Hegel gives some explanations on the theme of the freedom of the character-subject:

1. *The animal is entirely determined by its environment* — its basic needs for food, etc. — and therefore is not free. Man himself is unfree, to the extent that he is also, in part, an animal. The exterior needs experienced by man, the material needs, are a limitation on the exercise of his freedom. For this reason, the best characters for dramatic poetry, according to Hegel, are those who least feel the pressure of material needs. Princes, for example, who do not need to work physically to earn their living and who have multitudes of men at their disposal who can satisfy their material needs, are thus able to *freely externalize their spiritual impulses*. According to Hegel, all those many people who create for the prince the best conditions for his becoming a dramatic character, do not themselves qualify for that role — they are not good material for drama. . . .

2. Nor is a highly civilized society the type most likely to contribute good dramatic material, since the characters must appear as essentially free, able to determine their own fate, while the men of a developed society are tied hand and foot to all types of laws, customs, traditions, institutions, etc., and in this legal jungle cannot easily exert their freedom. In effect, if Hamlet had

been afraid of the police, the courts, lawyers, public prosecutors, etc., perhaps he would not have externalized the free impulses of his spirit by killing Polonius, Laertes, and Claudius. And, according to Hegel, the dramatic character needs all his freedom, by George!

3. But it must be noted, too, that freedom does not refer fundamentally to the "physical" aspect. Prometheus, for example, is a free man (excuse me, a free god). He is chained on a mountain, powerless to ward off the crows that come to eat his liver, which is restored every day so that the next day the crows may come again to eat it, and Prometheus impotently watches this daily feast. But Prometheus *can* act. He has enough power to put an end to this atrocious punishment; he has only to repent before Zeus, the highest of the gods, and he will be forgiven. Prometheus' freedom consists in his being able to end his own torment the moment he chooses, but he decides, freely, not to do it.

Hegel also tells the story of a painting by Murillo which shows a mother about to spank her child, who defiantly continues to hold a banana in his hand, on the point of eating it. The difference between the physical power of mother and child does not prevent the child from having enough freedom to defy his more powerful mother. For that reason, one can write a work about a character who is in jail, provided that he has the spiritual freedom to choose.

There are other characteristics which are important for the construction of a dramatic work:

1. The freedom of the character should not be exercised with respect to the accidental, the least important, the contingent, but rather in those areas which are the most universal, the most rational, the most essential, the most significant for human life. The family, the country, the state, morality, society, etc., are interests worthy of the human spirit, and therefore of dramatic poetry.

2. Art in general and dramatic poetry in particular play with concrete realities and not with abstractions: it is therefore necessary that the *particular* be seen in the *universal*. Philosophy deals with abstractions, mathematics with numbers, but the theater deals with individuals. It is necessary, then, to show them in all their concretion.

3. Precisely because the general interests dealt with in the

theater are universal (and not, on the contrary, idiosyncratic characteristics), those motivating forces of the human spirit are ethically justifiable. That is, the individual will of a character is the concretion of a moral value, or of an ethical option. Example: the concrete desire of Creon not to allow the burial of Antigone's brother is, in terms of individual will, the concretion of ethical intransigence in defense of the good of the State; the same can be said in relation to the iron will of Antigone in wanting to assure her brother's burial — that it is the concretion of a moral value, the good of the family. When these two individual wills clash, in reality two moral values collide. It is necessary for this conflict to end in repose, as Hegel views it, so that the moral dispute can be resolved: Who is right? Which is the greater value? In this particular case the conclusion shows that both moral values are right, though their expression may be exaggerated. The error is not in the value itself, but in its excess.

4. In order for tragedy to occur, if it is to be a true *tragedy,* the ends pursued by the characters must be irreconcilable; if a possibility of conciliation should exist, the dramatic work would belong to another genre, the *drama.*

Of all these Hegelian arguments, the one which most obviously characterizes his poetics is the one which insists on the character's nature as *subject;* that is, the argument that all exterior actions have their origin in the character's free spirit.

A Word Poorly Chosen

The Marxist poetics of Bertolt Brecht does not stand opposed to one or another formal aspect of the Hegelian idealist poetics but rather denies its very essence, asserting that the character *is not absolute subject* but the object of economic or social forces to which he responds and in virtue of which he acts.

If we were to make a logical analysis of a dramatic action typically belonging to Hegelian poetics, we would say that it is a simple sentence with subject, verb, and direct object. Example: "Kennedy invaded Girón Beach!" Here, the Hegelian subject is "Kennedy," whose inner spiritual impulses were externalized in the form of ordering the invasion of Cuba; "invade" is the verb and "Girón Beach" the direct object.

On the other hand, if it is with reference to a Marxist poetics of the type proposed by Brecht, the logical analysis would reveal the necessary presence of a main clause and a subordinate clause, in which "Kennedy" would continue to be the subject; but the subject of the main clause would be another. The sentence which would best explain the dramatic action, in this case, would be something like this: "Economic forces led Kennedy to invade Girón Beach." I believe that Bertolt Brecht's position is clear: the real subject is the economic forces which acted behind Kennedy. The main clause is always an interrelation of economic forces. The character *is not free* at all. He is an object-subject.

Now then, throughout Hegelian poetics — throughout and

not only in one of its parts — *the spirit is subject*. Epic poetry shows *actions determined by the spirit;* lyric poetry shows the *movements within that spirit itself;* finally, dramatic poetry presents, before our eyes, *the spirit and its actions in the exterior world.* Is this clear? The three genres of poetry entail the meeting of subjectivity and objectivity, but in every case it is always the subjectivity (the inner movements of the soul, the spirit) that produces the objectivity. This thought appears and reappears, is indeed constantly present, in Hegelian poetics.

In Brecht's objection, as well as in any other Marxist objection, what is at stake is who, or which term, precedes the other: the subjective or the objective. For idealist poetics, social thought conditions social being; for Marxist poetics, social being conditions social thought. In Hegel's view, the spirit creates the dramatic action; for Brecht, the character's social relations create the dramatic action.

Brecht is *squarely, totally, globally opposed* to Hegel. Therefore it is a mistake to use, for designating his poetics, a term which means a *genre* in the poetics of Hegel.

Brechtian poetics is not simply "epic": it is Marxist and, being Marxist, can be lyrical, dramatic, or epic. Many of his works belong to one genre, others to another, and still others to a third. Brecht's poetics embraces lyrical, as well as dramatic and epic works.

Brecht himself became aware of his initial mistake and, in his last writings, began to call his poetics, "dialectical poetics" — which is also a mistake, considering that Hegel's poetics, too, is dialectical. Brecht should have called his by its name: Marxist poetics! But at the time when he threw doubt on the initial designation, many books had already been written and the confusion was already established.

Utilizing now the outline of differences between idealist poetics and that of Brecht, an outline that he includes in his preface to *Mahagonny,* the following analysis is an attempt to point out which are the differences of genus and which are of species. In the outline we also include differences mentioned by Brecht in other works. It is not a "scientific" outline, and many of its terms are vague and imprecise. But if we keep in mind the fundamental difference — Hegel views the character as an absolute subject while Brecht sees him as object, as a spokesman for economic and social forces — if we keep this in mind, all the secondary differences will become clearer.

Some of the differences shown by Brecht actually refer more to differences between the epic, dramatic, and lyrical forms. They are:

1. Balance, subjectivity-objectivity;
2. Form of plot, whether or not it tends to the three unities;
3. Each scene does or does not determine, causally, the next scene;
4. Climactic rhythm, or linear narrative rhythm;
5. Curiosity for the denouement, or curiosity for the development; suspense, or scientific curiosity for a process;
6. Continuous evolution, or sporadic progression;
7. Suggestions, or argument?

Differences between the socalled "dramatic" and "epic" forms of theater, according to Brecht. (Outline based on the notes to *Mahagonny*, together with other writings.)[9]

The "Dramatic Form" according to Brecht. (Idealist Poetics).	The "Epic Form" according to Brecht. (Marxist Poetics).
1. Thought determines being. (Character-subject).	1. Social being determines thought. (Character-object).
2. Man is something given, fixed, inalterable, immanent, considered as known.	2. Man is alterable, object of the inquiry, and is "in process."
3. The conflict of free wills impels the dramatic action; the structure of the work is a scheme of wills in conflict.	3. Contradictions of economic, social, or political forces impel the dramatic action; the work is based on a structure of these contradictions.
4. It creates empathy, which consists in an emotional compromise of the spectator, depriving him of the possibility of acting.	4. It "historicizes" the dramatic action, transforming the spectator into observer, arousing his critical consciousness and capacity for action.
5. At the end, catharsis "purifies" the spectator.	5. Through knowledge, it drives the spectator to action.
6. Emotion.	6. Reason.
7. At the end, the conflict is resolved, and a new scheme of wills is created.	7. The conflict is left unresolved, and the fundamental contradiction emerges with greater clarity.
8. Hamartia prevents the character's adaptation to society, and this is the fundamental cause of the dramatic action.	8. The personal faults that the character may have are never the direct, fundamental cause of the dramatic action.
9. Anagnorisis justifies the society.	9. The knowledge acquired reveals the faults of the society.
10. It is action in the present.	10. It is narration.
11. Experience.	11. Vision of the world.
12. It arouses feelings.	12. It demands decisions.

Does Thought Determine Being
(or Vice Versa)?

As we have seen, in all the idealist poetics (Hegel, Aristotle, and others) the character is "born" with all his faculties and is already predisposed to feel and act in certain ways. His fundamental characteristics are immanent. On the other hand, for Brecht "human nature" does not exist, and therefore nobody is what he is "just because."

To clarify this difference, we can cite some examples from Brecht's works in which the action is determined by the character's social function. First, the classic example of the Pope carrying on a dialogue with Galileo Galilei and showing him his full sympathy and support while his aides dress him as Pope. When he finishes dressing, the Pope declares that even if from a personal point of view he might agree with Galileo, the latter will have to recant or answer to the Inquisition. The Pope, as long as he is Pope, acts as Pope.

Eisenhower proposed the invasion of Vietnam, Kennedy began to carry it out, and Johnson took it to genocidal extremes. Nixon, perhaps the greatest scoundrel of them all, was forced to make peace. Who is the criminal? The President of the United States of America: all, and any one, of them!

Another example: the good soul Shen Te, a very poor prostitute, suddenly receives a large inheritance and becomes a millionaire. Since she is very good, she cannot say "no" to all the friends, neighbors, relatives, and acquaintances who ask her for money. But as a very rich person, she decides to assume a new personality: she disguises herself as Shui Ta and pretends to be a cousin. Kindness and wealth cannot walk together. If a rich man could be kind, he would inevitably — out of kindness — give all his riches to the needy.

In the same play an aviator dreams poetically of the blue sky. But Shen Te (Shui Ta) offers him the enviable and well-paid position of foreman in a factory. Immediately the poetic pilot forgets the blue sky and only concerns himself with exploiting the workers more in order to obtain more profit.

Those are examples which show that social being, as Marx said, determines social thought. For this reason, the ruling classes pretend kindness and become reformist in critical moments; they give a little more meat and bread to the social beings who are workers, in the belief that a social being will be less revolutionary to the extent that he is less hungry. And this mechanism works. It is not for any other reason that the working classes in capitalist countries show so little revolutionary spirit, and rather prove to be reactionary, like the majority of the proletariat in the United States. They are social beings with refrigerators, cars, and houses who certainly do not have the same social thoughts as those Latin American beings who, by and large, live in slums, suffer hunger, and have no vestige of protection against disease and unemployment.

Can Man be Changed?

In *A Man is a Man* Brecht shows Galy Gay, a good man, whose parents' identity is unknown to him, an obedient being who leaves his house one morning to buy a fish for lunch. On his way he meets a patrol of three soldiers who have lost the fourth, without whom they cannot return to headquarters. They take hold of Galy Gay and make him sell an elephant to an old woman, in order to compromise him. Since he does not have an elephant handy, two of the soldiers disguise themselves as the animal. The old woman agrees to buy the elephant, for which she pays a certain sum, and poor Galy Gay becomes convinced that an elephant is anything a person may be inclined to buy as an elephant, as long as there is money. By selling it he commits an act of theft, since it was an elephant belonging to His Majesty.

Poor Galy Gay, who went to market one beautiful morning to buy a little fish, steals an elephant which is not an elephant, sells it to an old woman who is not a buyer, and in order not to be punished disguises himself as Jeriah Jip, changes into Jeriah Jip, and ends up as a war hero, attacking his enemies ferociously and asserting an atavic and ancestral thirst for blood. Before the spectators' eyes, says Brecht, a human being — a human "nature" — has been put together and taken apart.

For the sake of clarity we should point out that Brecht does not contend that the human being in other poetics is always unalterable. In Aristotle himself the hero ends up understanding his error, and he changes. But Brecht presents us with a broader, more total modification: Galy Gay is not Galy Gay; he does not exist purely and simply. Galy Gay is not Galy Gay, but rather is everything that Galy Gay is capable of doing in particular situations.

In his story "The Childhood of a Leader," Sartre shows a young man who by chance states that he does not like a certain person because that person is a Jew; it becomes known that he does not like Jews. At a party he is introduced to a certain man and, upon learning that he is a Jew, the future leader refuses to shake his hand. Later, the character becomes a rabid anti-Semite.

The procedures used by Sartre and Brecht have points in common, as well as differences. Common to both is the fact that neither the anti-Semitism of Sartre's young man nor the heroism of Galy Gay is immanent; these qualities are not born with the characters; they are not Aristotelian faculties transformed into passions and habits. Rather they are characteristics that happened to be acquired in social life. But there are fundamental differences: the leader evolves realistically through a sequence of causes and effects, while the Brechtian hero is dissected, disassembled, and reassembled. There is no realism here. It is an almost scientific demonstration carried out through artistic means.

Conflict of Wills or Contradiction of Needs?

As we have already seen, regardless of who the President of the United States of America may be, he will always have to defend the most reactionary imperalist interests. His individual will determines nothing. The action does not develop as it does because he is the person he is; it would develop in the same manner even if he were completely different.

It is necessary to clarify the possible confusion arising from the fact that Hegel also insists that the tragic conflict is an inevitability, a *necessity*. But while he does indeed speak of necessity, it is a necessity of a *moral* nature. That is, morally the characters cannot avoid being what they are and doing what they do. Brecht, on the other hand, does not speak of moral but of social or economic necessities. Mauler becomes good or bad, pardons or orders executions, not because of personal characteristics of kindness or evil, not because he thinks this way or that, but rather because he is a bourgeois who has to increase his profits more and more. When the wife of Dullfeet, murdered by Arturo Ui, meets the murderer, she feels the impulse to spit in his face, but she comes as a "proprietor," and ends up at his side — the two of them walking arm in arm with a very satisfied expression on their faces, following the casket of the dead man: the murderer and the widow are partners and so, what do their personal sentiments matter? They must love each other, always in search of profit!

Brecht does not mean to say that individual wills never intervene: what he wants to affirm is that they are never the determining factor of the fundamental dramatic action. In the last instance cited, for example, the young widow, at the beginning of the scene, lets her will run free; her hatred for Ui, as well as the whole scene, changes little by little as Ui demonstrates to her the inoperability of individual wills and the inflexible determination of social needs. The scene advances; the dramatic action develops through the contradiction of social needs (in this case, and almost always in capitalism it is a question of the desire for ever increasing profit).

Empathy or What? Emotion or Reason?

As we have seen in "Aristotle's Coercive System to Tragedy,"
empathy is the emotional relationship which is established between the character and spectator and which provokes, fundamentally, a delegation of power on the part of the spectator, who
becomes an object in relation to the character: whatever happens
to the latter, happens vicariously to the spectator.

In the case of Aristotle, the empathy he recommends consists in the emotional tie which involves two basic emotions: pity
and fear. The first binds us (the spectators) to a character who
suffers a tragic fate that is undeserved, given his great virtues,
and the second refers to the fact that that character suffers the
consequences of possessing some fault which we also possess.

But empathy does not necessarily refer only to those two
emotions — it can be realized through many other emotions, too.
The only indispensable element in empathy is that the spectator
assumes a "passive" attitude, delegating his ability to act. But
the emotion or emotions which provoke that phenomenon can be
any — fear (e.g., seeing films about vampires), sadism, sexual
desire for the star, or whatever.

We should note, furthermore, that already in Aristotle empathy did not appear alone, but simultaneously with another type
of relation: dianoia (character's thought-spectator's thought).
That is, empathy was the result of the ethos, but the action of
dianoia also provoked the action of a relation which John Gassner
called "enlightenment."

What Brecht asserts is that in idealist works the emotion acts by and for itself, producing what he calls "emotional orgies," while a materialist poetics — whose objective is not only that of interpreting the world but also of transforming it and making this earth finally habitable — has the obligation of showing how the world can be transformed.

A good empathy does not prevent understanding and, on the contrary, needs understanding precisely in order to avoid the spectacle's turning into an emotional orgy and the spectator's purging of his social sin. What Brecht does, fundamentally, is to place the emphasis on understanding (enlightment), on dianoia.

At no time does Brecht speak against emotion, though he always speaks against the emotional orgy. He says that it would be absurd to deny emotion to modern science, thus clearly indicating that his position is entirely favorable to that emotion which is born of pure knowledge, as opposed to the emotion which is born out of ignorance. Before a dark room from which a scream is hear, a child becomes frightened: Brecht is against any attempts to move the spectator with scenes of this type. But if Einstein discovers that $E = mc_2$, the formula of the transformation of matter into energy, what an extraordinary emotion! Brecht is totally in favor of this type of emotion. Learning is an emotional experience, and there is no reason to avoid such emotions. But at the same time, ignorance causes emotions, and one must oppose emotions of this kind!

How can one fail to be moved when Mother Courage loses her sons, one by one, in the war? Inevitably, the spectator is moved to tears. But the emotion caused by ignorance must be avoided. let no one weep over the "fate" that took Mother Courage's sons from her! Let one cry rather with anger against war and against the commerce of war, because it is this commerce that takes away the sons of Mother Courage.

Another comparison may help to clarify the distinction: there is a remarkable parallel between *Riders to the Sea*, by the Irishman J. M. Synge, and *Señora Carrar's Rifles*. The two works are tremendously moving. The stories are very similar: two mothers whose sons are lost at sea. In Synge's work the sea itself is the murderer; the waves, fate. In Brecht, it is the soldiers who shoot innocent fishermen. Synge's work produced a violent emotion, caused by the sea — unknown, impenetrable, fateful;

Brecht's work arouses a deep emotion of hatred against Franco and his fascist followers! In both cases emotion is produced, but of different colors, for different reasons, and with different results.

We must emphasize: What Brecht does *not* want is that the spectators continue to leave their brains with their hats upon entering the theater, as do bourgeois spectators.

Catharsis and Repose, or Knowledge and Action?

As we remarked previously, Hegel maintains that the tumult of human passions and actions making up the dramatic work is followed by a state of repose. Aristotle likewise speaks of a system of wills that represent concretely, individually, the justifiable ethical values, and which come into conflict because one of the characters possesses a tragic flaw, or commits a tragic error. After the catastrophe, when the flaw is purged, serenity returns necessarily; equilibrium is re-established. The two philosophers seem to say that the world returns to its perennial stability, its infinite equilibrium, its eternal repose.

Brecht was a Marxist; therefore, for him, a theatrical work cannot end in repose, in equilibrium. It must, on the contrary, show the ways in which society loses its equilibrium, which way society is moving, and how to hasten the transition.

Brecht contends that the popular artist must abandon the downtown stages and go to the neighborhoods, because only there will he find people who are truly interested in changing society: in the neighborhoods he should show his images of social life to the workers who are interested in changing that social life, since they are its victims.[10] A theater that attempts to change the changers of society cannot lead to repose, cannot re-establish equilibrium. The bourgeois police tries to re-establish equilibrium, to enforce repose: a Marxist artist, on the other hand, must promote the movement toward national liberation and toward the liberation of the classes oppressed by capital. Hegel and Aristotle see theater as a purging of the spectator's "antiestablishment" characteristics; Brecht clarifies concepts, reveals truths, exposes contradictions, and proposes transformations. The former desire a quiet somnolence at the end of the spectacle; Brecht wants the theatrical spectacle to be the beginning of action: the equilibrium should be sought by transforming society, and not by purging the individual of his just demands and needs.

In this respect, it is worthwhile to focus attention on the end of the play *Señora Carrar's Rifles*, referred to so many times as an "Aristotelian" work. Why is it described in this way? Because it is a realistic work, which conforms to the famous "three unities" of time, place, and action. But there all the supposed Aristotelian characteristics of the work end.

To assert that *Señora Carrar's Rifles* is Aristotelian because the heroine is "purged" of a flaw, is to argue falsely, evading the essence of the problem. Therefore we must repeat: catharsis takes away from the character (and thus from the spectator, who is empathically manipulated by the character) his ability to act. That is, it takes away pride, haughtiness, unilateralness in the love for the gods, etc., which are conducive to attitudes favorable to social change. Carrar, however, purges herself of non-action. Her lack of knowledge prevented her from acting in favor of a just cause, and consequently she desired the neutrality in which she believed and attempted to abstain from action by refusing to offer the rifles that were in her possession.

The Greek tragic character loses his propensity to act. Señora Carrar, on the contrary, becomes actively engaged in the civil war, because, while anagnorisis justifies society, the acquired knowledge here reveals the flaws, not of the character, but those of the society which must be changed. Hence Brecht's assertion that the idealist theater arouses feelings while the Marxist theater demands decisions. Señora Carrar makes a decision and starts to act; therefore, she is not Aristotelian.

How to Interpret the New Works?

Rather than attempting to explain at length the spectator-character relation proposed by Brecht to replace the relation of an emotional, paralyzing nature — which he condemned in the German bourgeois theater (or the bourgeois theater of any other nationality) — we quote below a portion of a poem he wrote in 1930, "On the Everyday Theatre":

> Look — the man at the corner re-enacting
> The accident.
> This he gives the driver at his wheel
> To the crowd for trial.
> Thus the victim, who seems old.
> Of each he only gives so much
> That the accident be understood
> Yet each lives before your eyes
> And each he presents in a manner
> To suggest the accident avoidable.
> So the event is understood
> And yet can still astound:
> The moves of both could have been different.
> Now he shows how both could have moved
> To circumvent the accident.
> This witness is free from superstition.
> Never to the stars
> Does he abandon his mortals
> But only to make their own mistakes.

Notice too
How serious and careful his imitation.
He knows that much depends on his precision:
Whether the innocent is ruined,
Whether the injured one receives his compensation.
See him now do what he has already done
Over again.
He hesitates,
Calls on his memory's aid,
Doubts if his imitation is truly good,
Stops to demand correction for this detail or that.
Observe with reverence.
And observe with astonishment:
This imitator never loses himself in his imitation.
Never does he lend himself whole
To the person he plays.
He remains, disengaged, the one who shows.
The man he represents has not confided in him.
Nor does he share
The feelings or views of this man.
He knows but little of him.
His imitation does not engender
A third
Composed in roughly equal parts
Of him and the other,
A third in whom but one heart beats
And one brain thinks.
His senses collected he, the performer,
Stands and gives us
The man next door,
A stranger.
In your theatres
You would take us in
With your magical transformation
Somewhere between
Dressing room and stage:
An actor leaves his room
A king enters the play,
And at this I've seen the stage hands
Laugh out loud with their bottles of beer.
Our performer there on the corner
Spins no such spell.
He's no sleep-walker you may not address,
Nor high priest at service.

Interrupt as you will.
Calmly he will reply
And when you have had your say
Continue his performance.
Don't declare this man is not an artist.
By creating this distinction between the world and yourselves
You banish yourselves from the world.
If you declare:
He is no artist,
He may reply:
You are not men.
A worse reproach by far.
Delcare instead:
He is an artist because a man.[11]

The poem continues and says much more. But we have quoted enough to suit our purpose here: the poem clarifies very well the differences between the bourgeois artist-high priest, elite artist, the unique individual (who, precisely because he is unique, can be sold at a better price: the star, whose name appears before the title of the work, before the subject and theme, before the contents of what is going to be seen) — and, by contrast, the other artist, the man: the man, who because he is a man, is capable of being what men are capable of being. Art is immanent to *all* men, and not only to a select few; art is not to be sold, no more than are breathing, thinking, loving. Art is not merchandise. But for the bourgeoisie everything is a commodity: man is a commodity. And this being so, all the things that man produces will likewise be commodities. Everything is prostituted in the bourgeois system, art as well as love. Man is the supreme prostitute of the bourgeoisie!

The Rest Does Not Count:
They Are Minor Formal Differences
Between the Three Genres.

The other differences pointed out by Brecht between his proposed conception of theater and the conceptions generally accepted in his time are in fact differences between the three possible genres of poetry.

For example, with regard to the balance between subjectivity
and objectivity, also in the poetics of Brecht one can find a
predominance of the objective (epic), the subjective (lyrical), or
an equilibrium of the two (dramatic). In the latter case, it is obvious that characters such as Mother Courage, Señora Carrar,
Galileo Galilei, Mauler, and other "dramatic" characters are objects of economic forces at work in reality and, in turn, they
themselves act upon reality. On the other hand, characters such
as Coolie or the Merchant of *The Exception and the Rule*, the
companions of *He Who Says Yes*, Galy Gay, Shui Ta of the *The
Good Woman of Setzuan*, and others, are characters in which the
function of objective spokesman clearly predominates: the subjectivity of these characters is atrophied in favor of clarity in the
exposition. At the opposite extreme, subjectivity prevails without
restraint in the lyrical characters of *In the Jungle of Cities* and of
other works still expressionistic. Expressionism "expresses" the
real subjectively, without showing it.

As for the tendency to concentrate action, time, and place —
observed by Brecht in previous poetics — this is true only with
respect to previous *dramatic* works. Literary works of a lyrical,

expressionistic, or surrealistic type, for example, do not tend to conform to that pattern, and neither did the Shakespearean and Elizabethan plays in general. While the concentration to which Brecht refers is proper only to the dramatic genre, and is totally absent from the lyrical and epic genres, it is furthermore proper to the dramatic genre *in both poetics* — idealist and materialist, Hegelian and Marxist.

All the other characteristics that Brecht points to belong likewise to the dramatic *genre*, and not to Hegelian or Brechtian *poetics*. Continuous evolution, or movement by leaps? It cannot be said that the development of Strindberg's *Lucky Peter's Journey* is a continuous one, with its surrealistic characters changing into animals or such things. And what is to be said of films like *The Cabinet of Dr. Caligari, Metropolis,* etc.? Often the idealist plays of a highly subjective style lose their ties with credibility, with objectivity; it is a tendency inherent in those styles, and which in surrealism reaches a paroxysm of no compromise with the objective world. Likewise, with reference to the causal relation of one scene to the following one, this indeed holds true for dramatic, but not for epic or lyrical works.

The outline of Brecht's poetics points up a scientific curiosity for the process rather than a morbid curiosity for the denouement. And this is true, but one has to take it in a relative sense: we cannot say that there is no curiosity regarding the outcome of the trial of Azdak (With whom will the child remain at last? Who is his *true* mother?). Morbid curiosity is found in its plenitude (and to an exclusive extent) only in mystery novels *a la* Agatha Christie or films *a la* Hitchcock, with or without vampires. In the same way that there is suspense in Azdak's trial or in the death of Mother Courage's mute daughter, *An Enemy of the People* arouses an intense scientific curiosity for the development of the liberal bourgeois mechanisms. Brecht fought for the acceptance of a new poetics and therefore necessarily radicalized his positions and statements. But those necessarily radical positions have to be understood dialectically because Brecht himself was the first to do the contrary, of what he himself preached, provided it was necessary. I repeat: provided it was necessary.

Another item in the outline cited above is also rather imprecise: suggestions or arguments? Brecht does not mean that, before him, no other author had utilized arguments, but only

suggestions, in his work. To understand Brecht more clearly
here, we should recall that in his view the artist's duty consists
not in showing true things but in revealing how things truly are.
And how is this to be done? And for whom is it to be done?
No one can answer these questions better than Brecht himself.
". . . I cannot say that the dramatic writing which I call 'non-
Aristotelian,' and the epic style of acting that goes with it, represent the only solution. However, one thing has become quite
plain: the present-day world can only be described to present-day
people if it is described *as capable of transformation.*"[12] And
furthermore: "It is in the interest of the people, the broad working masses, that literature should give them truthful representations of life; and truthful representations of life are in fact only
of use to the broad working masses, the people; so that they have
to be suggestive and intelligible to them, i.e. popular."[13]

Empathy or Osmosis

Empathy must be understood as the terrible weapon it really is. Empathy is the most dangerous weapon in the entire arsenal of the theater and related arts (movies and TV).

Its mechanism (sometimes insidious) consists in the juxtaposition of two people (one fictitious and another real), two universes, making one of those two people (the real one, the spectator) surrender to the other (the fictitious one, the character) his power of making decisions. The *man* relinquishes his power of decision to the *image*.

But here there is something monstrous: when man chooses, he does so in a real, vital situation, in his own life; when the character chooses (and therefore when he induces man to choose), he does so in a fictitious, unreal situation, lacking all the density of facts, nuances, and complications that life offers. This makes man (the real one) choose according to unreal situations and criteria.

The juxtaposition of two universes (the real and the fictitious) also produces other aggressive effects: *the spectator experiences the fiction and incorporates its elements*. The spectator — a real, living person — accepts as life and reality what is presented to him in the work of art as art. Esthetic osmosis.

Let us consider some concrete examples. The universe of Donald Duck's Uncle Scrooge is filled with money, with problems caused by money, and with the eagerness to acquire and keep money. Uncle Scrooge, being a likable character, establishes an empathic relation with the readers or with the spectators of the films (cartoons) in which he appears. Because of that empathy, because of the phenomenon of the juxtaposition of two universes, the spectators begin to experience as real, as their own, those desires for profit, that propensity to sacrifice everything for money. The audience adopts the rules of the game, as it does in playing any game.

In movies of the Old West, undoubtedly the ability to handle a gun and the skill in breaking a plate in flight with a single shot, or in knocking out ten bad men with a few punches, create the deepest empathy between those cowboys and the young spectators at the matinees. This occurs even in the case of a Mexican audience watching the Mexicans being knocked out while defending their land. Through empathy the children abandon their own universe, the need to defend what is theirs, and incorporate, empathically, the Yankee invader's universe, with his desire to conquer the lands of others.

Empathy functions even when there is a conflict of interests between the fictitious universe and the actual one of the spectators. That is why there is censorship: to prevent an undesirable universe from being juxtaposed to the spectators' universe.

A love story, no matter how simple it may be, can be the vehicle of the values of another universe which is not that of the spectator. I am convinced that Hollywood has done more damage to our countries with the "innocent" movies than with those that deal directly with more or less political themes. Idiotic love stories of the type of *Love Story* are more dangerous, given the fact that their ideological penetration takes place subliminally; the romantic hero works untiringly to win the woman's love, the bad boss reforms and becomes good (and goes on being the boss), etc.

The most recent success in American television, "Sesame Street," is obvious proof of American "solidarity" in relation to our poor, underdeveloped countries. Our North American neighbors want to help us to become educated, and they lend us their educational methods. But how do they educate? Showing a universe in which children learn. What do they learn? Letters, words, etc., of course. The learning experience is based on little sketches which show children learning how to use money, how to save money in their piggy banks, and learning the differences between a piggy bank and the bank downtown. Subjects and themes selected from among the values of a competitive capitalistic society. The little, defenseless spectators are exposed to that competitive, organized, coherent, and coercive world. That is how they educate us. By osmosis!

Notes for Chapter 3

[1]G. W. F. Hegel, *The Philosophy of Fine Art*, trans. F. P. B. Osmaston, 4 vols. (London: G. Bell and Sons, Ltd., 1920), 1:102-10.

[2]Hegel, 4:100.

[3]Hegel, 4:102.

[4]Hegel, 4:103.

[5]Hegel, 4:103-04.

[6]Hegel, 4:249.

[7]Hegel, 4:251.

[8]Hegel, 4:259-60.

[9]See Bertolt Brecht, *Brecht on Theatre*, ed. and trans. John Willett (New York: Hill and Wang, 1964), espec. p. 37.

[10]*Brecht on Theatre*, pp. 274-75.

[11]Bertolt Brecht, *Poems on the Theatre*, trans. John Berger and Anna Bostock (Lowestoft, Suffolk: Scorpion Press, 1961), pp. 6-7.

[12]*Brecht on Theatre*, p. 274. Italics added.

[13]*Brecht on Theatre*, p. 107.

Poetics of the Oppressed

Poetics of the Oppressed

In the beginning the theater was the dithyrambic song: free people singing in the open air. The carnival. The feast.

Later, the ruling classes took possession of the theater and built their dividing walls. First, they divided the people, separating actors from spectators: people who act and people who watch — the party is over! Secondly, among the actors, they separated the protagonists from the mass. The coercive indoctrination began!

Now the oppressed people are liberated themselves and, once more, are making the theater their own. The walls must be torn down. First, the spectator starts acting again: invisible theater, forum theater, image theater, etc. Secondly, it is necessary to eliminate the private property of the characters by the individual actors: the "Joker" System.

With the two essays that follow I attempt to close the circle of this book. In them we see some of the ways by which the people reassume their protagonistic function in the theater and in society.

Experiments with the People's Theater in Peru

These experiments were carried out in August of 1973, in the cities of Lima and Chiclayo, with the invaluable collaboration of Alicia Saco, within the program of the Integral Literacy Operation *(Operación Alfabetización Integral* [ALFIN]), directed by Alfonso Lizarzaburu and with the participation, in the various sectors, of Estela Liñares, Luis Garrido Lecca, Ramón Vilcha, and Jesús Ruiz Durand. The method used by ALFIN in the literacy program was, of course, derived from Paulo Freire.

In 1973, the revolutionary government of Peru began a national literacy campaign called *Operación Alfabetización Integral* with the objective of eradicating illiteracy within the span of four years. It is estimated that in Peru's population of 14 million people, between three and four million are illiterate or semi-illiterate.

In any country the task of teaching an adult to read and write poses a difficult and delicate problem. In Peru the problem is magnified because of the vast number of languages and dialects spoken by its people. Recent studies point to the existence of at least 41 dialects of the two principal languages, besides Spanish, which are the Quechua and the Aymara. Research carried out in the province of Loreto in the north of the country, verified the existence of 45 different languages in that region. Forty-five *languages,* not mere dialects! And this is what is perhaps the least populated province in the country.

This great variety of languages has perhaps contributed to an understanding on the part of the organizers of ALFIN, that the illiterate are not people who are unable to express themselves: they are simply people unable to express themselves in a particular language, which in this case is Spanish. All idioms are "languages," but there is an infinite number of languages that are not idiomatic. There are many languages besides those that are written or spoken. By learning a new language, a person acquires a new way of knowing reality and of passing that knowledge on to others. Each language is absolutely irreplaceable. All languages complement each other in achieving the widest, most complete knowledge of what is real.[1]

Assuming this to be true, the ALFIN project formulated two principal aims:

1) to teach literacy in both the first language and in Spanish without forcing the abandonment of the former in favor of the latter;

2) to teach literacy in all possible languages, especially the artistic ones, such as theater, photography, puppetry, films, journalism, etc.

The training of the educators, chosen from the same regions where literacy was to be taught, was developed in four stages according to the special characteristics of each social group:

1) *barrios* (neighborhoods) or new villages, corresponding to our slums *(cantegril, favela, . . .):*

2) rural areas;

3) mining areas;

4) areas where Spanish is not the first language, which embrace 40 percent of the population. Of this 40 percent, half is made up of bilingual citizens who learned Spanish after acquiring fluency in their own indigenous language. The other half speaks no Spanish.

It is too early to evaluate the results of the ALFIN plan since it is still in its early stages. What I propose to do here is to relate my personal experience as a participant in the theatrical sector and to outline the various experiments we made in considering the theater as language, capable of being utilized by any person, with or without artistic talent. We tried to show in practice how the theater can be placed at the service of the oppressed, so that they can express themselves and so that, by using this new language, they can also discover new concepts.

In order to understand this *poetics of the oppressed* one must keep in mind its main objective: to change the people — "spectators," passive beings in the theatrical phenomenon — into subjects, into actors, transformers of the dramatic action. I hope that the differences remain clear. Aristotle proposes a poetics in which the spectator delegates power to the dramatic character so that the latter may act and think for him. Brecht proposes a poetics in which the spectator delegates power to the character who thus acts in his place but the spectator reserves the right to think for himself, often in opposition to the character. In the first case, a "catharsis" occurs; in the second, an awakening of critical consciousness. But the *poetics of the oppressed* focuses on the action itself: the spectator delegates no power to the character (or actor) either to act or to think in his place; on the contrary, he himself assumes the protagonic role, changes the dramatic action, tries out solutions, discusses plans for change — in short, trains himself for real action. In this case, perhaps the theater is not revolutionary in itself, but it is surely a rehearsal for the revolution. The liberated spectator, as a whole person, launches into action. No matter that the action is fictional; what matters is that it is action!

I believe that all the truly revolutionary theatrical groups should transfer to the people the means of production in the theater so that the people themselves may utilize them. The theater is a weapon, and it is the people who should wield it.

But how is this transference to be achieved? As an example I cite what was done by Estela Linares, who was in charge of the photography section of the ALFIN Plan.

What would be the old way to utilize photography in a literacy project? Without doubt, it would be to photograph things, streets, people, landscapes, stores, etc., then show the pictures and discuss them. But who would take these pictures? The instructors, group leaders, or coordinators. On the other hand, if we are going to give the people the means of production, it is necessary to hand over to them, in this case, the camera. This is what was done in ALFIN. The educators would give a camera to members of the study group, would teach them how to use it, and propose to them the following:

We are going to ask you some questions. For this purpose we will speak in Spanish. And you must answer us. But you can not speak in Spanish: you must speak in "photography." We ask you things in

Spanish, which is a language. You answer us in photography, which is also a language.

The questions asked were very simple, and the answers — that is, the photos — were discussed later by the group. For example, when people were asked, where do you live?, they responded with the following types of photo-answers:

1) A picture showing the interior of a shack. In Lima it rarely rains and for this reason the shacks are made of straw mats, instead of with more permanent walls and roofs. In general they have only one room that serves as kitchen, living room, and bedroom; the families live in great promiscuity and very often young children watch their parents engage in sexual intercourse, which commonly leads to sexual acts between brothers and sisters as young as ten or eleven years old, simply as an imitation of their parents. A photo showing the interior of a shack fully answers the question, where do you live? Every element of each photo has a special meaning, which must be discussed by the group: the objects focused on, the angle from which the picture is taken, the presence or absence of people in it, etc.

2) To answer the same question, a man took a picture of the bank of a river. The discussion clarified its meaning. The river Rímac, which passes through Lima, overflows at certain times of the year. This makes life on its banks extremely dangerous, since shacks are often swept away, with a consequent loss of human lives. It is also very common for children to fall into the river while playing and the rising waters make rescue difficult. When a man answers the question with that picture, he is fundamentally expressing anguish: how can he work with peace of mind knowing that his child may be drowning in the river?

3) Another man photographed a part of the river where pelicans come to eat garbage in times of great hunger; the people, equally hungry, capture, kill and eat the pelicans. Showing this photo, the man communicated his awareness of living in a place where ironically the people welcomed hunger, because it attracted the pelicans which then served to satisfy their hunger.

4) A woman who had recently emigrated from a small village in the interior answered with a picture of the main street in her *barrio*: the old natives of Lima lived on one side of the street, while those from the interior lived on the other. On one side were those who saw their jobs threatened by the newcomers; on the

other, the poor who had left everything behind in search of work. The street was a dividing line between brothers equally exploited, who found themselves facing each other as if they were enemies. The picture helped to reveal their common condition: poverty on both sides — while pictures of the wealthier neighborhoods showed who were their true enemies. The picture of the divided street showed the need to redirect their violent resentment. . . . Studying the picture of her street helped the woman to understand her own reality.

5) One day a man, in answer to the same question, took a picture of a child's face. Of course everyone thought that the man had made a mistake and repeated the question to him:

"You didn't understand; what we want is that you show us where you live. Take a picture and show us where you live. Any picture; the street, the house, the town, the river. . . "

"Here is my answer. Here is where I live."

"But it's a child. . . ."

"Look at his face: there is blood on it. This child, as all the others who live here, have their lives threatened by the rats that infest the whole bank of the river Rímac. They are protected by dogs that attack the rats and scare them away. But there was a mange epidemic and the city dog-catcher came around here catching lots of dogs and taking them away. This child had a dog who protected him. During the day his parents used to go to work and he was left with his dog. But now he doesn't have it any more. A few days ago, when you asked me where I lived, the rats had come while the child was sleeping and had eaten part of his nose. This is why there's so much blood on his face. Look at the picture; it is my answer. I live in a place where things like this still happen."

I could write a novel about the children of the *barrios* along the river Rímac; but only photography, and no other language, could express the pain of that child's eyes, of those tears mixed with blood. And, as if the irony and outrage were not enough, the photograph was in Kodachrome, "Made in U.S.A."

The use of photography may help also to discover valid symbols for a whole community or social group. It happens many times that well intentioned theatrical groups are unable to communicate with a mass audience because they use symbols that are meaningless for that audience. A royal crown may symbolize power, but a symbol only functions as such if its meaning is shared. For some a royal crown may produce a strong impact and yet be meaningless for others.

What is exploitation? The traditional figure of Uncle Sam is, for many social groups throughout the world, the ultimate symbol of exploitation. It expresses to perfection the rapacity of "Yankee" imperialism.

In Lima the people were also asked, what is exploitation? Many photographs showed the grocer; others the landlord; still others, some government office. On the other hand, a child answered with the picture of a nail on a wall. For him that was the perfect symbol of exploitation. Few adults understood it, but all the other children were in complete agreement that the picture expressed their feelings in relation to exploitation. The discussion explained why. The simplest work boys engage in at the age of five or six is shining shoes. Obviously, in the *barrios* where they live there are no shoes to shine and, for this reason, they must go to downtown Lima in order to find work. Their shine-boxes and other tools of the trade are of course an absolute necessity, and yet these boys cannot be carrying their equipment back and forth every day between work and home. So they must rent a nail on the wall of some place of business, whose owner charges them two or three *soles* per night and per nail. Looking at a nail, those children are reminded of oppression and their hatred of it; the sight of a crown, Uncle Sam, or Nixon, however, probably means nothing to them.

It is easy enough to give a camera to someone who has never taken a picture before, tell him how to focus it and which button to press. With this alone the means of photographic production are in the hands of that person. But what is to be done in the case of the theater?

The means for producing a photograph are embodied in the camera, which is relatively easy to handle, but the means of producing theater are made up of man himself, obviously more difficult to manage.

We can begin by stating that the first word of the theatrical vocabulary is the human body, the main source of sound and movement. Therefore, to control the means of theatrical production, man must, first of all, control his own body, know his own body, in order to be capable of making it more expressive. Then he will be able to practice theatrical forms in which by stages he frees himself from his condition of spectator and takes on that of actor, in which he ceases to be an object and becomes a subject, is changed from witness into protagonist.

The plan for transforming the spectator into actor can be systematized in the following general outline of four stages:

First stage: *Knowing the body:* a series of exercises by which one gets to know one's body, its limitations and possibilities, its social distortions and possibilities of rehabilitation.

Second stage: *Making the body expressive:* a series of games by which one begins to express one's self through the body, abandoning other, more common and habitual forms of expression.

Third stage: *The theater as language:* one begins to practice theater as a language that is living and *present,* not as a finished product displaying images from the past:

First degree: *Simultaneous dramaturgy:* the spectators "write" simultaneously with the acting of the actors;

Second degree: *Image theater:* the spectators intervene directly, "speaking" through images made with the actors' bodies;

Third degree: *Forum theater:* the spectators intervene directly in the dramatic action and act.

Fourth stage: *The theater as discourse:* simple forms in which the spectator-actor creates "spectacles" according to his need to discuss certain themes or rehearse certain actions.

Examples:

1) *Newspaper theater*
2) *Invisible theater*
3) *Photo-romance theater*
4) *Breaking of repression*
5) *Myth theater*
6) *Trial theater*
7) *Masks and Rituals*

First Stage: Knowing the Body.

The initial contact with a group of peasants, workers, or villagers — if they are confronted with the proposal to put on a theatrical performance — can be extremely difficult. They have quite likely never heard of theater and if they have heard of it, their conception of it will probably have been distorted by television, with its emphasis on sentimentality, or by some traveling circus group. It is also very common for those people to associate theater with leisure or frivolity. Thus caution is required even when the contact takes place through an educator who belongs to the same class as the illiterates or semi-illiterates, even if he lives among them in a shack and shares their comfortless life. The very fact that the educator comes with the mission of eradicating illiteracy (which presupposes a coercive, forceful action) is in itself an alienating factor between the agent and the local people. For this reason the theatrical experience should begin not with something alien to the people (theatrical techniques that are taught or imposed) but with the *bodies* of those who agree to participate in the experiment.

There is a great number of exercises designed with the objective of making each person aware of his own body, of his bodily possibilities, and of deformations suffered because of the type of work he performs. That is, it is necessary for each one to feel the "muscular alienation" imposed on his body by work.

A simple example will serve to clarify this point: compare the muscular structure of a typist with that of the night watchman of a factory. The first performs his or her work seated in a chair: from the waist down the body becomes, during working hours, a kind of pedestal, while arms and fingers are active. The watchman, on the other hand, must walk continually during his eight-hour shift and consequently will develop muscular structures that facilitate walking. The bodies of both become alienated in accordance with their respective types of work.

The same is true of any person whatever the work or social status. The combination of roles that a person must perform imposes on him a "mask" of behavior. This is why those who perform the same roles end up resembling each other: artists, soldiers, clergymen, teachers, workers, peasants, landlords, decadent noblemen, etc.

Compare the angelical placidity of a cardinal walking in heavenly bliss through the Vatican Gardens with, on the other hand, an aggressive general giving orders to his inferiors. The former walks softly, listening to celestial music, sensitive to colors of the purest impressionistic delicacy: if by chance a small bird crosses the cardinal's path, one easily imagines him talking to the bird and addressing it with some amiable word of Christian inspiration. By contrast, it does not befit the general to talk with little birds, whether he cares to or not. No soldier would respect a general who talks to the birds. A general must talk as someone who gives orders, even if it is to tell his wife that he loves her. Likewise, a military man is expected to use spurs, whether he be a brigadier or an admiral. Thus all military officers resemble each other, just as do all cardinals; but vast differences separate generals from cardinals.

The exercises of this first stage are designed to "undo" the muscular structure of the participants. That is, to take them apart, to study and analyze them. Not to weaken or destroy them, but to raise them to the level of consciousness. So that each worker, each peasant understands, sees, and feels to what point his body is governed by his work.

If one is able, in this way, to disjoint one's own muscular structures, one will surely be able to assemble structures characteristic of other professions and social classes; that is, one will be able to physically "interpret" characters different from oneself.

All the exercises of this series are in fact designed to disjoint. Acrobatic and athletic exercises that serve to create muscular structures characteristic of athletes or acrobats are irrelevant here. I offer the following as examples of disjunctive exercises:

1) *Slow motion race.* The participants are invited to run a race with the aim of losing: the last one is the winner. Moving in slow motion, the body will find its center of gravity dislocated at each successive moment and so must find again a new muscular structure which will maintain its balance. The participants must never interrupt the motion or stand still; also they must take the longest step they can and their feet must rise above knee level. In this exercise, a 10-meter run can be more tiring than a conventional 500-meter run, for the effort needed to keep one's balance in each new position is intense.

2) *Cross-legged race.* The participants form pairs, embrace each other and interwine their legs (the left of one with the right of the other, and vice versa). In the race, each pair acts as if it were a single person and each person acts as if his mate were his leg. The "leg" doesn't move alone: it must be put in motion by its mate!

3) *Monster race.* "Monsters" of four legs are formed: each

person embraces the thorax of his mate but in reverse position; so that the legs of one fit around the neck of the other, forming a headless monster with four legs. The monsters then run a race.

4) *Wheel race.* The pairs form wheels, each one grabbing the ankles of the other, and run a race of human wheels.

5) *Hypnosis.* The pairs face each other and one puts his hand a few centimeters from the nose of his partner, who must keep this distance: the first one starts to move his hand in all directions, up and down, from left to right, slowly or faster, while the other moves his body in order to maintain the same distance between his nose and his partner's hand. During these movements he is forced to assume bodily positions that he never takes in his daily life, thus reforming permanently his muscular structures.

Later, groups of three are formed: one leads and the other two follow, one at each hand of the leader. The latter can do anything — cross his arms, separate his hands, etc., while the other two must try to maintain the distance. Afterward, groups of five are formed, one as leader and the other four keeping the distance in relation to the two hands and feet of the leader, while the latter can do what he pleases, even dance, etc.

6) *Boxing match.* The participants are invited to box, but they cannot touch each other under any circumstances; each one must fight as if he were really fighting but without touching his partner, who nevertheless must react as if he had received each blow.

7) *Out West.* A variation of the preceding exercises. The participants improvise a scene typical of bad western movies, with the pianist, the swaggering young cowboy, the dancers, the drunks, the villains who come in kicking the saloon doors, etc. The whole scene is performed in silence; the participants are not allowed to touch each other, but must react to every gesture or action. For example, an *imaginary* chair is thrown against a row of bottles (also imaginary), the pieces of which fly in all directions, and the participants react to the chair, the falling bottles, etc. At the end of the scene all must engage in a free-for-all fight.

All these exercises are included in my book *200 Exercises and Games for the Actor and for the Non-actor Who Wants to Say Something Through Theater.* There are many more exercises that can be used in the same manner. In proposing exercises it's always advisable to ask the participants to describe or invent others: in this stage, the type that would serve to analyze the muscular structures of each participant. At every stage, however, the maintenance of a creative atmosphere is extremely important.

Second Stage: Making the Body Expressive.

In the second stage the intention is to develop the expressive ability of the body. In our culture we are used to expressing everything through words, leaving the enormous expressive capabilities of the body in an underdeveloped state. A series of "games" can help the participants to begin to use their bodily resources for self-expression. I am talking about parlor games and not necessarily those of a theatrical laboratory. The participants are invited to "play," not to "interpret," characters but they will "play" better to the extent that they "interpret" better.

For example: In one game pieces of paper containing names of animals, male and female, are distributed, one to each participant. For ten minutes, each person tries to give a physical, bodily impression of the animal named on his piece of paper. Talking or making noises that would suggest the animal is forbidden. The communication must be effected entirely through the body. After the first ten minutes, each participant must find his mate among the others who are imitating the animals, since there will always be a male and a female for each one. When two participants are convinced that they constitute a pair, they leave the stage, and the game is over when all participants find their mates through a purely physical communication, without the utilization of words or recognizable sounds.

What is important in games of this type is not to guess right but rather that all the participants try to express themselves through their bodies, something they are not used to doing. Without realizing it they will in fact be giving a "dramatical performance."

I remember one of these games played in a slum area, when a man drew the name *hummingbird*. Not knowing how to express it physically, he remembered nevertheless that this bird flies very rapidly from one flower to another, stops and sucks on a flower while producing a peculiar sound. So with his hands the man imitated the frenetic wings of the hummingbird and, "flying" from participant to participant, halted before each one of them making that sound. After ten minutes, when it was time for him to look for his mate, this man looked all around him and found no one who seemed to be enough of a hummingbird to attract him. Finally he saw a tall, fat man who was making a pendular movement with his hands and, setting aside his doubts, decided that there was his beloved mate; he went straight to "her," making turns around "her" and throwing little kisses to the air while singing joyfully. The fat man, upset, tried to escape, but the other fellow went after him, more and more in love with his hummingbird mate and singing with ever more amorous glee. Finally, though convinced that the other man was not his mate, the fat one — while the others roared with laughter — decided to follow his persistent suitor off stage simply to end the ordeal. Then (for only then were they allowed to talk) the first man, full of joy, cried out:

"I am the male hummingbird, and you are the female? Isn't that right?"

The fat one, very discouraged, looked at him and said: "No, dummy, I'm the bull. . . ."

How the fat man could give an impression of a delicate hummingbird while trying to portray a bull, we will never know. But, no matter: what does matter is that for 15 or 20 minutes all those people tried to "speak" with their bodies.

This type of game can be varied *ad infinitum;* the slips of paper can bear, for example, the names of occupations or professions. If the participants depict an animal, it will perhaps have little to do with their ideology. But if a peasant is called upon to act as a landlord; a worker, the owner of a factory; or if a woman must portray a policeman, all their ideology counts and finds physical expression through the game. The names of the participants themselves may be written on slips of paper, requiring them to convey impressions of each other and thus revealing, physically, their opinions and mutual criticisms.

In this stage, as in the first, regardless of how many games one proposes to the participants, the latter should always be encouraged to invent other games and not to be passive recipients of an entertainment that comes from the outside.

Third Stage: The Theater as Language:

This stage is divided into three parts, each one representing a different degree of direct participation of the spectator in the performance. The spectator is encouraged to intervene in the action, abandoning his condition of object and assuming fully the role of subject. The two preceding stages are preparatory, centering around the work of the participants with their own bodies. Now this stage focuses on the theme to be discussed and furthers the transition from passivity to action.

First degree: *Simultaneous dramaturgy:* This is the first invitation made to the spectator to intervene without necessitating his physical presence on the "stage."

Here it is a question of performing a short scene, of ten to twenty minutes, proposed by a local resident, one who lives in the *barrio*. The actors may improvise with the aid of a script prepared beforehand, as they may also compose the scene directly. In any case, the performance gains in theatricality if the person who proposed the theme is present in the audience. Having begun the scene, the actors develop it to the point at which the main problem reaches a crisis and needs a solution. Then the actors stop the performance and ask the audience to offer solutions. They improvise immediately all the suggested solutions, and the audience has the right to intervene, to correct the actions or words of the actors, who are obligated to comply strictly with these instructions from the audience. Thus, while the audience "writes" the work the actors perform it simultaneously. The spectator's thoughts are discussed theatrically on stage with the help of the actors. All the solutions, suggestions, and opinions are revealed in theatrical form. The discussion itself need not simply take the form of words, but rather should be effected through all the other elements of theatrical expression as well.

Here's an example of how simultaneous dramaturgy works. In a *barrio* of San Hilariòn, in Lima, a woman proposed a controversial theme. Her husband, some years before, had told her to keep some "documents" which, according to him, were extremely important. The woman — who happened to be illiterate — put them away without suspicion. One day they had a fight for one reason or another and, remembering the documents, the woman decided to find out what they were all about, since she was afraid they had something to do with the ownership of their small house. Frustrated in her inability to read, she asked a neighbor to read the documents to her. The lady next door kindly made haste to read the documents, which to the surprise and amusement of the whole *barrio*, were not documents at all, but rather love letters written by the mistress of the poor woman's husband. Now this betrayed and illiterate woman wanted revenge. The actors improvised the scenes until the moment when the husband returns home at night, after his wife has uncovered the mystery of the letters. The woman wants revenge: how is she to get it? Here the action is interrupted and the participant who was interpreting the woman asked the others what should be her attitude in relation to her husband.

All the women of the audience entered into a lively exchange of views. The actors listened to the different suggestions and acted them out according to instructions given by the audience. All the possibilities were tried. Here are some of the suggested solutions in this particular case:

1) To cry a lot in order to make him feel guilty. One young woman suggested that the betrayed woman start to cry a lot so that the husband might feel bad about his own behavior. The actress carried out this suggestion: she cried a lot, the husband consoled her, and when the crying was over he asked her to serve his dinner; and everything remained as it was before. The husband assured her that he had already forgotten the mistress, that he loved only his wife, etc., etc. The audience did not accept this solution.

2) To abandon the house, leaving her husband alone as a punishment. The actress carried out this suggestion and, after reproaching her husband for his wicked behavior, grabbed her things, put them in a bag, and left him alone, very lonely, so that he would learn a lesson. But upon leaving the house (that is, her own house), she asked the public about what she should do next. In punishing her husband she ended up punishing herself. Where would she go now? Where could she live? This punishment positively was not good since it turned against the punisher, herself.

3) To lock the house so that the husband would have to go away. This variation was also rehearsed. The husband repeatedly begs to be let in, but the wife steadfastly refused. After insisting several times, the husband commented:

"Very well, I'll go away. They paid me my salary today, so I'll take the money and go live with my mistress and you can just get by the best way you can." And he left. The actress commented that she did not like this solution, since the husband went

to live with the other woman, and what about the wife? How is
she going to live now? The poor woman does not make enough
money to support herself and cannot get along without her
husband.

4) The last solution was presented by a large, exuberant
woman; it was the solution accepted unanimously by the entire
audience, men and women. She said: "Do it like this: let him
come in, get a really big stick, and hit him with all your might —
give him a good beating. After you've beat him enough for him to
feel repentant, put the stick away, serve him his dinner with
affection, and forgive him. . . ."

The actress performed this version, after overcoming the
natural resistence of the actor who was playing the husband, and
after a barrage of blows — to the amusement of the audience —
the two of them sat at the table, ate, and discussed the latest
measures taken by the government, which happened to be the
nationalization of American companies.

This form of theater creates great excitement among the participants and starts to demolish the wall that separates actors
from spectators. Some "write" and others act almost simultaneously. The spectators feel that they can intervene in the action.
The action ceases to be presented in a deterministic manner, as
something inevitable, as Fate. Man is Man's fate. Thus Man-the-
spectator is the creater of Man-the-character. Everything is subject to criticism, to rectification. All can be changed, and at a
moment's notice: the actors must always be ready to accept,
without protest, any proposed action; they must simply act it out,
to give a live view of its consequences and drawbacks. Any
spectator, by virtue of being a spectator, has the right to try his
version — without censorship. The actor does not change his
main function: he goes on being the interpreter. What changes is
the object of his interpretation. If formerly he interpreted the
solitary author locked in his study, to whom divine inspiration
dictated a finished text, here on the contrary, he must interpret
the mass audience, assembled in their local committees, societies
of "friends of the barrio," groups of neighbors, schools, unions,
peasant leagues, or whatever; he must give expression to the
collective thought of men and women. The actor ceases to interpret the individual and starts to interpret the group, which is
much more difficult and at the same time much more creative.

Second degree: *Image theater:* Here the spectator has to participate more directly. He is asked to express his views on a certain theme of common interest that the participants wish to discuss. The theme can be far-reaching, abstract — as, for example, imperialism — or it can be a local problem such as the lack of water, a common occurrence in almost all the *barrios*. The participant is asked to express his opinion, but without speaking, using only the bodies of the other participants and "sculpting" with them a group of statues, in such a way that his opinions and feelings become evident. The participant is to use the bodies of the others as if he were a sculptor and the others were made of clay: he must determine the position of each body down to the most minute details of their facial expressions. He is not allowed to speak under any circumstances. The most that is permitted to him is to show with his own facial expressions what he wants the statue-spectator to do. After organizing this group of statues he is allowed to enter into a discussion with the other participants in order to determine if all agree with his "sculpted" opinion. Modifications can be rehearsed: the spectator has the right to modify the statues in their totality or in some detail. When finally an image is arrived at that is the most acceptable to all, then the spectator-sculptor is asked to show the way he would like the given theme to be; that is, in the first grouping the *actual image* is shown, in the second the *ideal image*. Finally he is asked to show a *transitional image*, to show how it would be possible to pass from one reality to the other. In other words, how to carry out the change, the transformation, the revolution, or whatever term one wishes to use. Thus, starting with a grouping of "statues" accepted by all as representative of a real situation, each one is asked to propose ways of changing it.

Once again, a concrete example can best clarify the matter. A young woman, a literacy agent who lived in the village of Otuzco, was asked to explain, through a grouping of live images, what her home town was like. In Otuzco, before the present Revolutionary Government,[2] there was a peasant rebellion; the landlords (that no longer exist in Peru), imprisoned the leader of the rebellion, took him to the main square, and, in front of everyone, castrated him. The young woman from Otuzco composed the image of the castration, placing one of the participants on the ground while another pretended to be castrating him and still another held him from behind. Then at one side she placed a woman praying, on her knees, and at the other side a group of five men and women, also on their knees, with hands tied behind their backs. Behind the man being castrated, the young woman placed another participant in a position obviously suggestive of power and violence and, behind him, two armed men pointing their guns at the prisoner.

This was the image that person had of her village. A terrible, pessimistic, defeatist image, but also a true reflection of something that had actually taken place. Then the young woman was asked to show what she would want her village to be like. She modified completely the "statues" of the group and regrouped them as people who worked in peace and loved each other — in short, a happy and contented, ideal Otuzco. Then came the third, and most important part, of this form of theater: how can one, starting with the actual image, arrive at the ideal image? How to bring about the change, the transformation, the revolution?

Here it was a question of giving an opinion, but without words. Each participant had the right to act as a "sculptor" and to show how the grouping, or organization, could be modified through a reorganization of forces for the purpose of arriving at an ideal image. Each one expressed his opinion through imagery. Lively discussions arose, but without words. When one would exclaim, "It's not possible like this; I think that . . .," he was immediately interrupted: "Don't say what you think; come and show it to us." The participant would go and demonstrate physically, visually, his thought, and the discussion would continue. In this particular case the following variations were observed:

1) When a young woman from the interior was asked to form the image of change, she would never change the image of the kneeling woman, signifying clearly that she did not see in that woman a potential force for revolutionary change. Naturally the young women identified themselves with that feminine figure and, since they could not perceive themselves as possible protagonists of the revolution, they left unmodified the image of the kneeling woman. On the other hand, when the same thing was asked of a girl from Lima, she, being more "liberated," would start off by changing precisely that image with which she identified herself. This experiment was repeated many times and always produced the same results, without variation. Undoubtedly the different

patterns of action represent not chance occurrence but the sincere, visual expression of the ideology and psychology of the participants. The young women from Lima always modified the image: some would make the woman clasp the figure of the castrated man, others would prompt the woman to fight against the castrator, etc. Those from the interior did little more than allow the woman to lift her hands in prayer.

2) All the participants who believed in the Revolutionary Government would start by modifying the armed figures in the background: they changed the two men who were aiming their guns at the victim so that they would then aim at the powerful figure in the center or at the castrators themselves. On the other hand, when a participant did not have the same faith in his government, he would alter all figures except the armed ones.

3) The people who believed in magical solutions or in a "change of conscience" on the part of the exploiting classes, would start by modifying the castrators — viewing them in effect as changing of their own volition — as well as the powerful figure in the center, who would become regenerated. By contrast, those who did not believe in this form of social change would first alter the kneeling men, making them assume a fighting posture, attacking the oppressors.

4) One of the young women, besides showing the transformations to be the work of the kneeling men — who would free themselves, attack their torturers and imprison them — also had one of the figures representing the people address the other participants, clearly expressing her opinion that social changes are made by the people as a whole and not only by their vanguard.

5) Another young woman made all kinds of changes, leaving untouched only the five persons with their hands tied. This girl belonged to the upper middle class. When she showed signs of nervousness for not being able to imagine any further changes, someone suggested to her the possibility of changing the group of tied figures; the girl looked at them in surprise and exclaimed: "The truth is that those people didn't fit in! . . ." It was the truth. The people did not fit into her view of the scheme of things, and she had never before been able to see it.

This form of image theater is without doubt one of the most stimulating, because it is so easy to practice and because of its extraordinary capacity for making thought *visible*. This happens because use of the language idiom is avoided. Each word has a denotation that is the same for all, but it also has a connotation that is unique for each individual. If I utter the word "revolution," obviously everyone will realize that I am talking about a radical change, but at the same time each person will think of his or her "own" revolution, a personal conception of revolution. But if I have to arrange a group of statues that will signify "my revolution," here there will be no denotation-connotation dichotomy. The image synthesizes the individual connotation and the collective denotation. In my arrangement signifying revolution, what are the statues doing? Do they have weapons in their hands or do they have ballots? Are the figures of the people united in a fighting posture against the figures representing the common enemies; or are the figures of the people dispersed, or showing disagreement among themselves? My conception of "revolution" will become clear if, instead of speaking, I show with images what I think.

I remember that in a session of psychodrama a girl spoke repeatedly of the problems she had with her boyfriend, and she always started with more or less the same phrase: "He came in, embraced me, and then. . . ." Each time we heard this opening phrase we understood that they did in fact embrace; that is, we understood what the word *embrace* denotes. Then one day she showed by acting how their meetings were: he approached, she crossed her arms over her breasts as if protecting herself, he took hold of her and hugged her tightly, while she continued to keep her hands closed, defending herself. That was clearly a particular connotation for the word *embrace*. When we understood her "embrace" we were finally able to understand her problems with her boyfriend.

In image theater other techniques can be used:

1) Each participant transformed into a statue is allowed one movement or gesture, and only one, each time a signal (like a clap of hands) is given. In this case the arrangement of images will change according to the individual desire of each participant.

2) The participants are first asked to memorize the ideal image, then to return to the original, actual image, and finally to make the movements necessary to arrive again at the ideal image — thus showing the group of images in motion and allowing the analysis of the feasibility of the proposed transitions. One will

then be able to see if change occurs by the grace of God or if it is brought about by the opposing forces operating within the very core of the group.

3) The sculptor-participant, once his work is finished, is asked to try to place himself in the group he has created. This sometimes helps the person to realize that his own vision of reality is a cosmic one, as if he were a part of that reality.

The game of images offers many other possibilities. The important thing is always to analyze the feasibility of the change.

Third degree: *Forum theater:* This is the last degree and here the participant has to intervene decisively in the dramatic action and change it. The procedure is as follows: First, the participants are asked to tell a story containing a political or social problem of difficult solution. Then a ten- or fifteen-minute skit portraying that problem and the solution intended for discussion is improvised or rehearsed, and subsequently presented. When the skit is over, the participants are asked if they agree with the solution presented. At least some will say no. At this point it is explained that the scene will be performed once more, exactly as it was the first time. But now any participant in the audience has the right to replace any actor and lead the action in the direction that seems to him most appropriate. The displaced actor steps aside, but remains ready to resume action the moment the participant considers his own intervention to be terminated. The other actors have to face the newly created situation, responding instantly to all the possibilities that it may present.

The participants who choose to intervene must continue the physical actions of the replaced actors; they are not allowed to come on the stage and talk, talk, talk: they must carry out the same type of work or activities performed by the actors who were in their place. The theatrical activity must go on in the same way, on the stage. Anyone may propose any solution, but it must be done on the stage, working, acting, doing things, and not from the comfort of his seat. Often a person is very revolutionary when in a public forum he envisages and advocates revolutionary and heroic acts; on the other hand, he often realizes that things are not so easy when he himself has to practice what he suggests.

An example: An eighteen-year-old man worked in the city of Chimbote, one of the world's most important fishing ports. There are in that city a great number of factories of fish meal, a principal export product of Peru. Some factories are very large, while others have only eight or nine employees. Our young man worked for one of the latter. The boss was a ruthless exploiter and forced his employees to work from eight o'clock in the morning to eight at night, or vice versa — twelve consecutive hours of work. Thus the problem was how to combat this inhuman exploitation. Each participant had a proposal: one of them was, for example, "operation turtle," which consists in working very slowly, especially when the boss is not looking. Our young man had a brilliant idea: to work faster and fill the machine with so much fish that it would break with the excessive weight, requiring two or three hours to fix it. During this time the workers could rest. There was the problem, the employer's exploitation; and there was one solution, invented by native ingenuity. But would that be the best solution?

The scene was performed in the presence of all the participants. Some actors represented the workers, another represented the boss, another the foreman, another a "stool pigeon." The stage was converted into a fish meal factory: one worker unloading the fish, another weighing the bags of fish, another carrying the bags to the machines, another tending the machine, while still others performed other pertinent tasks. While they worked, they kept up a dialogue, proposing solutions and discussing them until they came to accept the solution proposed by the young man and broke the machine; the boss came and the workers rested while the engineer repaired the machine. When the repair was done, they went back to work.

The scene was staged for the first time and the question was raised: Were all in agreement? No, definitely not. On the contrary, they disagreed. Each one had a different proposal: to start a strike, throw a bomb at the machine, start a union, etc.

Then the technique of forum theater was applied: the scene would be staged exactly as it had been the first time, but now each spectator-participant would have the right to intervene and change the action, trying out his proposal. The first to intervene was the one who suggested the use of a bomb. He got up, replaced the actor who was portraying the young man, and made his bomb-throwing proposal. Of course all the other actors argued against it since that would mean the destruction of the factory, and therefore the source of work. What would become of so many workers if the factory closed up? Disagreeing, the man decided to throw the bomb himself, but soon realized that he did not know how to manufacture a bomb nor even how to throw it. Many people who in theoretical discussions advocate throwing bombs would not know what to do in reality, and would probably be the first to perish in the explosion. After trying his bomb-solution, the man returned to his place and the actor replaced him until a second person came to try his solution, the strike. After much argument with the others he managed to convince them to stop working and walk out, leaving the factory abandoned. In this case, the owner, the foreman, and the "stool pigeon," who had remained in the factory, went to the town square (among the audience) to look for other workers who would replace the strikers (there is mass unemployment in Chimbote). This spectator-participant tried his solution, the strike, and realized its impracticability; with so much unemployment the bosses would always be able to find workers hungry enough and with little enough political consciousness to replace the strikers.

The third attempt was to form a small union for the purpose of negotiating the workers' demands, politicizing the employed workers, as well as the unemployed, setting up mutual funds, etc. In this particular session of forum theater, this was the solution judged to be the best by the participants. In the forum theater no idea is imposed: the audience, the people, have the opportunity to try out all their ideas, to rehearse all the possibilities, and to verify them in practice, that is, in theatrical practice. If the audience had come to the conclusion that it was necessary to dynamite all the fish meal factories in Chimbote, this would also be right from their point of view. It is not the place of the theater to show the correct path, but only to offer the means by which all possible paths may be examined.

Maybe the theater in itself is not revolutionary, but these theatrical forms are without a doubt a *rehearsal of revolution*. The truth of the matter is that the spectator-actor practices a real act even though he does it in a fictional manner. While he *rehearses* throwing a bomb on stage, he is concretely rehearsing the way a bomb is thrown; acting out his attempt to organize a strike, he is concretely organizing a strike. Within its fictitious limits, the experience is a concrete one.

Here the cathartical effect is entirely avoided. We are used to plays in which the characters make the revolution on stage and the spectators in their seats feel themselves to be triumphant revolutionaries. Why make a revolution in reality if we have already made it in the theater? But that does not happen here: the rehearsal stimulates the practice of the act in reality. Forum theater, as well as these other forms of a people's theater, instead of taking something away from the spectator, evoke in him a desire to practice in reality the act he has rehearsed in the theater. The practice of these theatrical forms creates a sort of uneasy sense of incompleteness that seeks fulfillment through real action.

Fourth Stage: The Theater as Discourse.

George Ikishawa used to say that the bourgeois theater is the finished theater. The bourgeoisie already knows what the world is like, *their* world, and is able to present images of this complete, finished world. The bourgeoisie presents the spectacle. On the other hand, the proletariat and the oppressed classes do not know yet what their world will be like; consequently their theater will be the rehearsal, not the finished spectacle. This is quite true, though it is equally true that the theater can present images of transition.

I have been able to observe the truth of this view during all my activities in the people's theater of so many and such different countries of Latin America. Popular audiences are interested in experimenting, in rehearsing, and they abhor the "closed" spectacles. In those cases they try to enter into a dialogue with the actors, to interrupt the action, to ask for explanations without waiting politely for the end of the play. Contrary to the bourgeois code of manners, the people's code allows and encourages the spectator to ask questions, to dialogue, to participate.

All the methods that I have discussed are forms of a rehearsal-theater, and not a spectacle-theater. One knows how these experiments will begin but not how they will end, because the spectator is freed from his chains, finally acts, and becomes a protagonist. Because they respond to the real needs of a popular audience they are practiced with success and joy.

But nothing in this prohibits a popular audience from practicing also more "finished" forms of theater. In Peru many forms previously developed in other countries, especially Brazil and Argentina, were also utilized and with great success. Some of these forms were:

1) *Newspaper theater.* It was initially developed by the Nucleus Group of the Arena Theater of Sao Paulo, of which I was the artistic director until forced to leave Brazil.[3] It consists of several simple techniques for transforming daily news items, or any other non-dramatic material, into theatrical performances.

a) Simple reading: the news item is read detaching it from the context of the newspaper, from the format which makes it false or tendentious.

b) Crossed reading: two news items are read in crossed (alternating) form, one throwing light on the other, explaining it, giving it a new dimension.

c) Complementary reading: data and information generally omitted by the newspapers of the ruling classes are added to the news.

d) Rhythmical reading: as a musical commentary, the news is read to the rhythm of the samba, tango, Gregorian chant, etc., so that the rhythm functions as a critical "filter" of the news, revealing its true content, which is obscured in the newspaper.

e) Parallel action: the actors mime parallel actions while the news is read, showing the context in which the reported event really occurred; one hears the news and sees something else that complements it visually.

f) Improvisation: the news is improvised on stage to exploit all its variants and possibilities.

g) Historical: data or scenes showing the same event in other historical moments, in other countries, or in other social systems, are added to the news.

h) Reinforcement: the news is read or sung with the aid or accompaniment of slides, jingles, songs, or publicity materials.

i) Concretion of the abstract: that which the news often hides in its purely abstract information is made concrete on the stage: torture, hunger, unemployment, etc., are shown concretely, using graphic images, real or symbolic.

j) Text out of context: the news is presented out of the context in which it was published; for example, an actor gives the speech about austerity previously delivered by the Minister of Economics while he devours an enormous dinner: the real truth behind the minister's words becomes demystified — he wants austerity for the people but not for himself.

2) *Invisible theater:* It consists of the presentation of a scene

in an environment other than the theater, before people who are not spectators. The place can be a restaurant, a sidewalk, a market, a train, a line of people, etc. The people who witness the scene are those who are there by chance. During the spectacle, these people must not have the slightest idea that it is a "spectacle," for this would make them "spectators."

The invisible theater calls for the detailed preparation of a skit with a complete text or a simple script; but it is necessary to rehearse the scene sufficiently so that the actors are able to incorporate into their acting and their actions the intervention of the spectators. During the rehearsal it is also necessary to include every imaginable intervention from the spectators; these possibilities will form a kind of optional text.

The invisible theater erupts in a location chosen as a place where the public congregates. All the people who are near become involved in the eruption and the effects of it last long after the skit is ended.

A small example shows how the invisible theater works. In the enormous restaurant of a hotel in Chiclayo, where the literacy agents of ALFIN were staying, together with 400 other people, the "actors" sit at separate tables. The waiters start to serve. The "protagonist" in a more or less loud voice (to attract the attention of other diners, but not in a too obvious way) informs the waiter that he cannot go on eating the food served in that hotel, because in his opinion it is too bad. The waiter does not like the remark but tells the customer that he can choose something *a la carte*, which he may like better. The actor chooses a dish called "Barbecue a la pauper." The waiter points out that it will cost him 70 *soles*, to which the actor answers, always in a reasonably loud voice, that there is no problem. Minutes later the waiter brings him the barbecue, the protagonist eats it rapidly and gets ready to get up and leave the restaurant, when the waiter brings the bill. The actor shows a worried expression and tells the people at the next table that his barbecue was much better than the food they are eating, but the pity is that one has to pay for it. . . .

"I'm going to pay for it; don't have any doubts. I ate the 'barbecue a la pauper' and I'm going to pay for it. But there is a problem: I'm broke."

"And how are you going to pay?," asks the indignant waiter." "You knew the price before ordering the barbecue. And now, how are you going to pay for it?"

The diners nearby are, of course, closely following the dialogue — much more attentively than they would if they were witnessing the scene on a stage. The actor continues: "Don't worry, because I *am* going to pay you. But since I'm broke I will pay you with labor-power."

"With what?," asks the waiter, astonished. "What kind of power?"

"With labor-power, just as I said. I am broke but I can rent you my labor-power. So I'll work doing something for as long as it's necessary to pay for my 'barbecue a la pauper,' which, to tell the truth, was really delicious — much better than the food you serve to those poor souls. . . ."

By this time some of the customers intervene and make remarks among themselves at their tables, about the price of food, the quality of the service in the hotel, etc. The waiter calls the headwaiter to decide the matter. The actor explains again to the latter the business of renting his labor-power and adds:

"And besides, there is another problem: I'll rent my labor-power but the truth is that I don't know how to do anything, or very little. You will have to give me a very simple job to do. For example, I can take out the hotel's garbage. What's the salary of the garbage man who works for you?"

The headwaiter does not want to give any information about salaries, but a second actor at another table is already prepared and explains that he and the garbage man have gotten to be friends and that the latter has told him his salary: seven *soles* per hour. The two actors make some calculations and the "protagonist" exclaims:

"How is this possible! If I work as a garbage man I'll have to work ten hours to pay for this barbecue that it took me ten minutes to eat? It can't be! Either you increase the salary of the garbage man or reduce the price of the barbecue!. . . But I can do something more specialized; for example, I can take care of the hotel gardens, which are so beautiful, so well cared for. One can see that a very talented person is in charge of the gardens. How much does the gardener of this hotel make? I'll work as a gardener! How many hours work in the garden are necessary to pay for the 'barbecue a la pauper'?"

A third actor, at another table, explains his friendship with the gardener, who is an immigrant from the same village as he; for this reason he knows that the gardener makes ten *soles* per hour. Again the "protagonist" becomes indignant: "How is this possible? So the man who takes care of these beautiful gardens, who spends his days out there exposed to the wind, the rain, and the sun, has to work seven long hours to be able to eat the barbecue in ten minutes? How can this be, Mr. Headwaiter? Explain it to me!"

The headwaiter is already in despair; he dashes back and forth, gives orders to the waiters in a loud voice to divert the attention of the other customers, alternately laughs and becomes serious, while the restaurant is transformed into a public forum. "The "protagonist" asks the waiter how much he is paid to serve the barbecue and offers to replace him for the necessary number of hours. Another actor, originally from a small village in the interior, gets up and declares that nobody in his village makes 70 *soles* per day; therefore nobody in his village can eat the "barbecue a la pauper." (The sincerity of this actor, who was, besides, telling the truth, moved those who were near his table.)

Finally, to conclude the scene, another actor intervenes with the following proposition:

"Friends, it looks as if we are against the waiter and the headwaiter and this does not make sense. They are our brothers. They work like us, and they are not to blame for the prices charged here. I suggest we take up a collection. We at this table are going to ask you to contribute whatever you can, one *sol,* two *soles,* five *soles,* whatever you can afford. And with that money we are going to pay for the barbecue. And be generous, because what is left over will go as a tip for the waiter, who is our brother and a working man."

Immediately those who are with him at the table start collecting money to pay the bill. Some customers willingly give one or two *soles.* Others furiously comment:

"He says that the food we're eating is junk, and now he wants us to pay for his barbecue! . . . And am I going to eat this junk? Hell no? I wouldn't give him a peanut, so he'll learn a lesson! Let him wash dishes. . . ."

The collection reached 100 *soles* and the discussion went on through the night. It is always very important that the actors do not reveal themselves to be actors! On this rests the *invisible* nature of this form of theater. And it is precisely this invisible quality that will make the spectator act freely and fully, as if he were living a real situation — and, after all, it is a real situation! It is necessary to emphasize that the invisible theater is not the same thing as a "happening" or the so-called "guerrilla theater." In the latter we are clearly talking about "theater," and therefore the wall that separates actors from spectators immediately arises, reducing the spectator to impotence: a spectator is always less than a man! In the invisible theater the theatrical rituals are abolished; only the theater exists, without its old, worn-out patterns. The theatrical energy is completely liberated, and the impact produced by this free theater is much more powerful and longer lasting.

Several presentations of invisible theater were made in different locations in Peru. Particularly interesting is what happened at the Carmen Market, in the *barrio* of Comas, some 14 kilometers away from downtown Lima. Two actresses were protagonists in a scene enacted at a vegetable stand. One of them, who was pretending to be illiterate, insisted that the vendor was cheating her, taking advantage of the fact that she did not know how to read; the other actress checked the figures, finding them to be correct, and advised the "illiterate" one to register in one of ALFIN's literacy courses. After some discussion about the best age to start one's studies, about what to study and with whom, the first actress kept on insisting that she was too old for those things. It was then that a little old woman, leaning on her cane, very indignantly shouted:

"My dears, that's not true? For learning and making love one is never too old!"

Everyone witnessing the scene broke into laughter at the old woman's amorous outburst, and the actresses were unable to continue the scene.

3) *Photo-romance:* In many Latin-American countries there is a genuine epidemic of photo-romances, sub-literature on the lowest imaginable level, which furthermore always serves as a vehicle for the ruling classes' ideology. The technique here consists in reading to the participants the general lines in the plot of a photo-romance without telling them the source of this plot. The participants are asked to act out the story. Finally, the acted-out story is compared to the story as it is told in the photo-romance,

and the differences are discussed.

For example: a rather stupid story taken from Corín Tellado, the worst author of this brutalizing genre, started like this:

A woman is waiting for her husband in the company of another woman who is helping her with the housework. . . . The participants acted according to their customs: a woman at home expecting her husband will naturally be preparing the meal; the one helping her is a neighbor, who comes to chat about various things; the husband comes home tired after a long day's work; the house is a one-room shack, etc., etc. In Corín Tellado, on the contrary, the woman is dressed in a long evening gown, with pearl necklaces, etc.; the woman who is helping her is a black maid who says no more than "Yes, ma'am"; "The dinner is served, ma'am"; "Very well, ma'am"; "Here comes Mr. X, ma'am"; and nothing else. The house is a marble palace; the husband comes home after a day's work in his factory, where he had an argument with the workers because they, "not understanding the crisis we are all living through, wanted an increase in salaries . . . ," and continuing in this vein.

This particular story was sheer trash, but at the same time it served as magnificent example of ideological insight. The well-dressed woman received a letter from an unknown woman, went to visit her, and discovered her to be a former mistress of her husband; the mistress stated that the husband had left her because he wanted to marry the factory owner's daughter, that is, the well-dressed woman. To top it all, the mistress exclaimed:

"Yes, he betrayed me, deceived me. But I forgive him because, after all, he has always been very ambitious, and he knew very well that with me he could not climb very high. On the other hand, with you he can go very far indeed!"

That is to say, the former mistress forgave her lover because he had in the highest degree that capitalistic eagerness to possess everything. The desire to be a factory owner is presented as something so noble that even a few betrayals on the way up are to be forgiven. . . .

And the young wife, not to be outdone, pretends to be ill so that he will have to remain at her side, and so that, as a result of this trick, he will finally fall in love with her. What an ideology! This love story is crowned with a happy ending rotten to the core. Of course the story, when told without the dialogues and acted out by peasants, takes on an entirely different meaning. When at the end of the performance, the participants are told the origin of the plot they have just acted out, they experience a shock. And this must be understood: when they read Corín Tellado they immediately assume the passive role of "spectators"; but if they first of all have to act out a story themselves, afterwards, when they do read Corín Tellado's version, they will no longer assume a passive, expectant attitude, but instead a critical, comparative one. They will look at the lady's house, and compare it to their own, at the husband's or wife's attitudes and compare them with those of their own spouses, etc. And they will be prepared to detect the poison infiltrating the pages of those photo-stories, or the comics and other forms of cultural and ideological domination.

I was overjoyed when, months after the experiments with the educators, back in Lima, I was informed that the residents of several *barrios* were using that same technique to analyze television programs, an endless source of poison directed against the people.

4) *Breaking of repression:* The dominant classes crush the dominated ones through repression; the old crush the young through repression; certain races subjugate certain others through repression. Never through a cordial understanding, through an honest interchange of ideas, through criticism and autocriticism. No. The ruling classes, the old, the "superior" races, or the masculine sex, have their sets of values and impose them by force, by unilateral violence, upon the oppressed classes, the young, the races they consider inferior, or women.

The capitalist does not ask the working man if he agrees that the capital should belong to one and the labor to another; he simply places an armed policeman at the factory door and that is that — private property is decreed.

The dominated class, race, sex, or age group suffers the most constant, daily, and omnipresent repression. The ideology becomes concrete in the figure of the dominated person. The proletariat is exploited through the domination that is exerted on all proletarians. Sociology becomes psychology. There is not an oppression by the masculine sex in general of the feminine sex in general: what exists is the concrete oppression that men (individuals) direct against women (individuals).

The technique of breaking repression consists in asking a participant to remember a particular moment when he felt especially repressed, accepted that repression, and began to act in a manner contrary to his own desires. That moment must have a deep personal meaning: I, a proletarian, am oppressed; we proletarians are oppressed; therefore the proletariat is oppressed. It is necessary to pass from the particular to the general, not vice versa, and to deal with something that has happened to someone in particular, but which at the same time is typical of what happens to others.

The person who tells the story also chooses from among the rest of the participants all the other characters who will participate in the reconstruction of the incident. Then, after receiving the information and directions provided by the protagonist, the participants and the protagonist act out the incident just as it happened in reality — recreating the same scene, the same circumstances, and the same original feelings.

Once the "reproduction" of the actual event is over, the protagonist is asked to repeat the scene, but this time without accepting the repression, fighting to impose his will, his ideas, his wishes. The other participants are urged to maintain the repression as in the first performance. The clash that results helps to measure the possibility one often has to resist and yet fails to do so; it helps to measure the true strength of the enemy. It also gives the protagonist the opportunity of trying once more and carrying out, in fiction, what he had not been able to do in reality. But we have already seen that this is not cathartic: the fact of having rehearsed a resistance to oppression will prepare him to resist effectively in a future reality, when the occasion presents itself once more.

On the other hand, it is necessary to take care that the generic nature of the particular case under study be understood. In this type of theatrical experiment the particular instance must serve as the point of departure, but it is indispensable to reach the general. The process to be realized, during the actual performance or afterward during the discussion, is one that ascends from the *phenomenon* toward the *law;* from the phenomena presented in the plot toward the social laws that govern those phenomena. The spectator-participants must come out of this experience enriched with the knowledge of those laws, obtained through analysis of the phenomena.

5) *Myth theater:* It is simply a question of discovering the obvious behind the myth: to logically tell a story, revealing its evident truths.

In a place called Motupe there was a hill, almost a mountain, with a narrow road that led through the trees to the top; halfway to the top stood a cross. One could go as far as that cross: to go beyond it was dangerous; it inspired fear, and the few who had tried had never returned. It was believed that some sanguinary ghosts inhabited the top of the mountain. But the story is also told of a brave young man who armed himself and climbed to the top, where he found the "ghosts." They were in reality some Americans who owned a gold mine located precisely on the top of that mountain.

Another legend is that of the lagoon of Cheken. It is said that there was no water there and that all the peasants, having to travel for several kilometers to get a glass of water, were dying of thirst. Today a lagoon exists there, the property of a local landowner. How did that lagoon spring up and how did it become the property of one man? The legend explains it. When there was still no water, on a day of intense heat all the villagers were lamenting and praying to God to grant them even a tiny stream of water. But God did not have pity on that arid village. At midnight of the same day, however, a man dressed in a long black poncho and riding a black horse arrived and addressed the landowner, who was then only a poor peasant like the others:

"I will give a lagoon for all of you, but *you,* friend, must give me your most precious possession."

The poor man, very distressed, moaned:

"But I have nothing; I am very poor. We all here suffer from the lack of water, live in miserable shacks, suffer from the most terrible hunger. We have nothing precious, not even our lives. And myself in particular, my only precious possession is my three daughters, nothing else."

"And of the three," responded the stranger, "the oldest is the most beautiful. I will give you a lagoon filled with the freshest water of all Peru; but in exchange you will give me your oldest daughter so that I may marry her."

The future landlord thought for a long while, cried a lot, and asked his frightened eldest daughter if she would accept such an unusual marriage proposal. The obedient daughter expressed herself in this way:

"If it is for the salvation of all, so that the thirst and hunger of all the peasants will come to an end, if it is so that you may have a lagoon with the freshest water of all Peru, if it is so that that lagoon will belong to you alone and bring you personal prosperity and riches — for you will be able to sell this wonderful water to the peasants, who will find it cheaper to buy from you than to travel so many kilometers — if it is for all this, tell the gentleman in the black poncho, astride his black horse, that I will go with him, even if in my heart I am suspicious of his true identity and of the places he will take me."

Happy and contented, and of course somewhat tearful, the kind father went to inform the man in black of the decision, meanwhile asking the daughter to make some little signs showing the price of a liter of water, in order to expedite the work. The man in black undressed the girl, for he did not want to take anything from that house besides the girl herself, and placed her on his horse, which set off at a gallop toward a great depression in the plains. Then an enormous explosion was heard, and a large cloud of smoke remained in the very place where the horse, horseman, and naked girl had disappeared. From the huge hole that had been made in the ground, a spring started to flow and formed the lagoon with the freshest water of all Peru.

This myth no doubt hides a truth: the landlord took possession of what did not belong to him. If formerly the noblemen attributed to God the granting of their property and rights, today explanations no less magical are still used. In this case, the property of the lagoon was explained by the loss of the eldest daughter, the landlord's most precious possession — a transaction took place! And serving as a reminder of that, the legend said that on the nights of the new moon one could hear the girl singing at the bottom of the lagoon, still naked and combing her long hair with a beautiful golden comb. . . . Yes, the truth is that for the landlord the lagoon was like gold.

The myths told by the people should be studied and analyzed and their hidden truths revealed. In this task the theater can be extraordinarily useful.

6) *Analytical theater:* A story is told by one of the participants and immediately the actors improvise it. Afterward each

character is broken down into all his social roles and the participants are asked to choose a physical object to symbolize each role. For example, a policeman killed a chicken thief. The policeman is analyzed:

a) he is a worker because he rents his labor-power; symbol: a pair of overalls;

b) He is a bourgeois because he protects private property and values it more than human life; symbol: a necktie, or a top hat, etc.;

c) he is a repressive agent because he is a policeman; symbol: a revolver.

This is continued until the participants have analyzed all his roles: head of a family (symbol: the wallet, for example), member of a fraternal order, etc., etc. It is important that the symbols be chosen by the participants present and that they not be imposed "from above." For a particular community the symbol for the head of the family might be a wallet, because he is the person who controls the household finances, and in this way controls the family. For another community this symbol may not communicate anything, that is, it may not be a symbol; then an armchair may be chosen. . . .

Having analyzed the character, or characters (it is advisable to limit this operation to the central characters only, for the sake of simplicity and clarity), a fresh attempt to tell the story is made, but taking away some of the symbols from each character, and consequently some social roles as well. Would the story be exactly the same if:

a) the policeman did not have the top hat or the necktie?

b) the robber had a top hat or necktie?

c) the robber had a revolver?

d) the policeman and the robber both had the same symbol for the fraternal order?

The participants are asked to make varying combinations and the proposed combinations must be performed by the actors and criticized by all those present. In this way they will realize that human actions are not the exclusive and primordial result of individual psychology: almost always, through the individual speaks his class!

7) *Rituals and masks:* The relations of production (infrastructure) determine the culture of a society (superstructure).

Sometimes the infrastructure changes but the superstructure for a while remains the same. In Brazil the landlords would not allow the peasants to look them in the face while talking with them: this would mean lack of respect. The peasants were accustomed to talking with the landlords only while staring at the ground and murmuring: "yes, sir; yes, sir; yes, sir." When the government decreed an agrarian reform (before 1964, date of the facist *coup d'etat*) its emissaries went to the fields to tell the peasants that now they could become landowners. The peasants, staring at the ground, murmured: "yes, friend; yes, friend; yes, friend." A feudalistic culture had totally permeated their lives. The relationships of the peasant with the landlord were entirely different from those with the agent of the Institute of Agrarian Reform, but the ritual remained unchanged.

This particular technique of a people's theater ("Rituals and masks") consists precisely in revealing the superstructures, the rituals which reify all human relationships, and the masks of behavior that those rituals impose on each person according to the roles he plays in society and the rituals he must perform.

A very simple example: a man goes to a priest to confess his sins. How will he do it? Of course, he will kneel, confess his sins, hear the penitence, cross himself, and leave. But do all men confess always in the same way before all priests? Who is the man, and who is the priest?

In this case we need two versatile actors to stage the same confession four times:

First scene: the priest and the parishioner are landlords;

Second scene: the priest is a landlord and the parishioner is a peasant;

Third scene: the priest is a peasant and the parishioner is a landlord;

Fourth scene: the priest and the parishioner are peasants.

The ritual is the same in each instance, but the different social masks will cause the four scenes to be different also.

This is an extraordinarily rich technique which has countless variants: the same ritual changing masks; the same ritual performed by people of one social class, and later by people of another class; exchange of masks within the same ritual; etc., etc.

Conclusion: "Spectator," a Bad Word!

Yes, this is without a doubt the conclusion: "Spectator" is a bad word! The spectator is less than a man and it is necessary to humanize him, to restore to him his capacity of action in all its fullness. He too must be a subject, an actor on an equal plane with those generally accepted as actors, who must also be spectators. All these experiments of a people's theater have the same objective — the liberation of the spectator, on whom the theater has imposed finished visions of the world. And since those responsible for theatrical performances are in general people who belong directly or indirectly to the ruling classes, obviously their finished images will be reflections of themselves. The spectators in the people's theater (i.e., the people themselves) cannot go on being the passive victims of those images.

As we have seen in the first essay of this book, the poetics of Aristotle is the *poetics of oppression:* the world is known, perfect or about to be perfected, and all its values are imposed on the spectators, who passively delegate power to the characters to act and think in their place. In so doing the spectators purge themselves of their tragic flaw — that is, of something capable of changing society. A catharsis of the revolutionary impetus is produced! Dramatic action substitutes for real action.

Brecht's poetics is that of the enlightened vanguard: the world is revealed as subject to change, and the change starts in the theater itself, for the spectator does not delegate power to the characters to think in his place, although he continues to delegate power to them to act in his place. The experience is revealing on the level of consciousness, but not globally on the level of the action. Dramatic action throws light upon real action. The spectacle is a preparation for action.

The *poetics of the oppressed* is essentially the poetics of liberation: the spectator no longer delegates power to the characters either to think or to act in his place. The spectator frees himself; he thinks and acts for himself! Theater is action!

Perhaps the theater is not revolutionary in itself; but have no doubts, it is a rehearsal of revolution!

Notes for Chapter 4

¹Chart of Various Languages

Communication of Reality	Substantiation of Reality	Transformation of Reality
Language	*Lexicon* (vocabulary)	*Syntax*
Spoken-written	Words	Sentence (subject, object, predicate, etc.)
Music	Musical instruments and their sounds (timbre, tonalities, etc.), notes	Musical phrase; melody and rhythm
Painting	Colors and forms	Each style has its syntax.
Cinema	Image (secondarily, music and speech)	Montage: splicing, superimposition, usage of lens, traveling, fade-in, fade-out, etc.
Theater	*Sum of all imaginable languages:* words, colors, forms, movements, sounds, etc.	*Dramatic action*

²The government established after the October 1968 revolution and headed by President Juan Velasco Alvarado (replaced in August 1975 by Francisco Morales Bermúdez). (Translators' note).

³Under the author's leadership the Arena Theater developed into one of Brazil's — indeed, one of Latin America's — most outstanding theaters. After 1964, when military rule was established in that country, Boal's work continued, though hampered by censorship and other restrictions imposed by the government. His outspoken position against the authoritarian regime led to his imprisonment and torture in 1971. Released after three months and acquitted of all charges, he was nevertheless compelled to leave Brazil in order to insure the safety of himself and his family. After political circumstances also forced him to leave Buenes Aires, Argentina, he took up residence in Portugal.

Development
of the
Arena Theater
of São Paulo

These articles were written in 1966 for the staging of the work *Arena conta Tiradentes (Arena tells about Tiradentes)*, by Augusto Boal and Gianfrancesco Guarnieri, music by Caetano Veloso, Gilberto Gil, Théo de Barros, and Sydney Miller, in the Arena Theater of São Paulo, Brazil.

First Stage

In 1956, the Arena Theater entered into its "realist" stage. Among its many characteristics, this stage signified a "no" to conventional theater. What was the state of the conventional theater? In that year the theatrical panorama of São Paulo was still dominated by the esthetics of TBC (Teatro Brasileiro de Comedia), a theater founded — and it was its founder who said it — between two glasses of whisky, and was the pride of the "fastest growing city." It was made by those who have money, to be seen also by those who have it. An indiscriminate luxury covers equally Gorki and Goldoni. A theater to show the world: "Here, too, good European theater is presented." "On parle français." "We are a distant province but we have an Old World soul."

It was the nostalgia for what was far away, but the joy of doing it almost in the same way. The Arena found out that we were far from the great cultural centers but close to ourselves and wanted to create a theater which would be close. Close to whom? To its public. And who was its public? Well, here begins another story. When the TBC appeared, the great stars of our stages were at the brink of ruin: actor-promotors who centered the whole spectacle around themselves, stepping majestically upon a pedestal of supporting cast and "N.N."[1] The public was unable to see the characters since the stars showed themselves to be always identical to themselves, regardless of the text. But the stars were few and were well-known.

The TBC broke with all that. Theater performed by a team: a new concept. The public returned to the theater to see what it was all about and mixed with the fans of stars. If the latter were the financial elite of São Paulo, the former was the middle class. In the beginning it was a happy marriage. But the incompatibility of character of the two publics immediately became evident. The first stage of the Arena came to answer the needs of that break and to satisfy the middle class. The latter tired of the abstract and beautiful stagings, and — rather than the impeccable British diction — preferred to see and hear Brazilian actors who, even if they were stutterers, would stutter in the Brazilian language, mixing the "tú" with "vós," and not in continental Portuguese.

The Arena had to answer with national texts and Brazilian performances. But there were no such works. The few national authors were preoccupied with Hellenic myths. Nelson Rodrigues was even lauded with the following phrase: "Nelson creates in Brazil, for the first time, a drama that reflects the true Greek tragic feeling of existence." We were interested in combating the Italianism of TBC but not at the price of becoming Hellenized. Therefore the only recourse left to us was to utilize modern realist texts, even though they were written by foreign authors.

Realism had other advantages, besides being easy to perform. If formerly the model of excellence was seen in a nearly perfect imitation of Gielgud, now we started to use the imitation of the reality visible around us. The interpretation was better to the extent that the actors were themselves and not simply actors.

In the Arena the Actor's Laboratory was founded. Stanislavski was minutely analyzed word by word and practiced from nine in the morning until it was time to appear on stage. Guarnieri, Oduvaldo Viana Filho, Flavio Misciaccio, Nelson Yarier, Milton Gonçalves, and others are the actors who gave a firm foundation to this period.

At that time the works selected were, among others: Steinbeck's *Of Mice and Men*, O'Casey's *Juno and the Paycock*, Sidney Howard's *They Knew What They Wanted*, and others which, though they were done later correspond esthetically to this period, such as *Señora Carrar's Rifles* by Brecht. The traditional stage and the circular differ in their adaptability. One might expect the traditional stage to be more appropriate for naturalism, since the circular stage always reveals the theatrical character of any performance: audience facing audience, with the actors in between, and all the theatrical mechanisms bared, without disguise — reflectors, entries and exits, rudimentary decorations. Surprisingly, the circular stage proved to be the better form for the realistic theater, since it is the only one which allows for the close-up technique: all spectators are close to all actors, the audience can smell the coffee being served on stage and observe the spaghetti as it is being swallowed. The "furtive tear" reveals its secret. The stage *a la italiana* always utilizes the long-shot.

As for the image, in one of his articles Guarnieri outlined the evolution of the stage at the Arena Theater, seeing it in three steps. First, the timid form wanted to pass for a conventional stage, showing structures of doors and windows. As image, the circular stage was no more than poor scenery. Second, the circular stage becomes aware of its autonomous form and demands absolute simplicity: some pieces of straw on the floor symbolize a haystack (or a barn), a brick is a wall, and the spectacle is concentrated on the actors' performance. Third, from that simplicity is born a scenic art appropriate to the form. The best example was the staging created by Flavio Imperio for *Child of the Turkey*.

The arrival of Flavio Imperio, who became a member of the team, introduced scenic art into the Arena.

With regard to the performance, the actor constituted the essence of the theatrical phenomenon; he was the demiurge of the theater — without him nothing was done. He summed up everything.

However, if before our peasants were transformed into Frenchmen by our "deluxe actors," now the Irish revolutionists were Brazilian villagers. The dichotomy continued, now inverted. What was absolutely necessary was a dramaturgy that would create Brazilian characters for our actors. The Seminar of Dramaturgy is founded in São Paulo.

In the beginning doubt prevailed: how would young people, with almost no experience either in life or on the stage, be transformed into playwrights? Some twelve of them got together, studied, discussed, wrote, and the second stage began.

Second Stage: Photography

It started in February of 1958. The first play produced was

They Don't Wear Tuxedos by G. Guarnieri, which ran for a whole year, until 1959. It represented the first appearance in our theater of the urban, proletarian drama.

During the four years that followed (until 1964) many beginning playwrights came to public attention: Oduvaldo Viana Filho *(Chapetuba F.C.)*, Roberto Freire *(People Like Us)*, Edy Lima *(The Farce of the Perfect Wife)*, Augusto Boal *(Revolution in South America)*, Flavio Migliaccio *(Painted Happy)*, Francisco de Assis *(The Bandit's Will)*, Benedito Rui Barbosa *(Cold Fire)*, and others.

It was a long period during which the Arena Theater closed its doors to European playwrights, regardless of their high quality, opening them to anyone who wished to talk about Brazil to a Brazilian audience.

This phase coincided with political nationalism, with the flourishing of industry in São Paulo, with the foundation of Brasília, with the euphoria of prizing highly everything that is national. At this time the Bossa Nova and the New Cinema were also born.

The plays dealt with anything that was Brazilian: bribery in provincial soccer games, strikes against capitalists, adultery in a small village, subhuman living conditions of railway employees, bandits *(cangaceiros)* in the Northeast, and popular belief in visions of the Holy Virgin and devils, etc.

The style varied little and bore some resemblance to photography, following too closely in the footsteps of the first success of the series. The peculiarities of life were the main theme of this dramatic cycle. And that was its main limitation: the audience always saw what was already familiar to them. They were delighted at first, to see on stage the next-door neighbor and the man on the street. Later they came to realize they could see them without buying a ticket.

The interpretation in this stage continued along the familiar path of the Stanislavski system. However, if the interpretative emphasis was placed previously on "feeling emotions," now the emotions became dialectic processes and the emphasis fell on the "flow of emotions." "No more lakes, but rather emotional rivers," if I may borrow a metaphor from Mao Tse-tung. The laws of dialectics were applied mechanically; the conflict of opposing wills was developed qualitatively and quantitatively within an interdependent conflictive structure. Thus Stanislavski was incorporated into a scheme. In spite of the Russian director's resistance to the incorporation, all his theories fitted into that scheme perfectly. This phase necessarily had to be superseded. Its advantages were great: Brazilian authors stopped being the box offices' terror, since almost all of them had successful plays produced. Inspired with enthusiasm by the existence of a theater which presented only national authors, many aspirants became playwrights, contributing with their works to the formation of a more Brazilian and less mimetic theater.

Third Stage: Nationalization of the Classics

We chose *Mandragola* by Machiavelli, in a translation by Mario da Silva. Machiavelli was the first ideologist of the then incipient bourgeoisie; our production was inserted into the century of its decadence.

And the ideologist of this last breath is Dale Carnegie. In fact, the maxims of these two thinkers are identical, in spite of being separated by four centuries of history. The "self-made man" of the decadent is the same "man of virtù" of the Florentine; in spite of the identity, the latter threatens while the former plays tricks.

Mandragola in our version was done not as an academic work, but as an outline still effective for the taking of political power. The power, in that tale, is symbolized by Lucrezia, the young wife kept under lock and key but, even so, still accessible to anyone who wants her and will fight for her, as long as one fights keeping in mind the desired end and not the morality of the means that are utilized.

After *Mandragola* came other classics: *The Novice*, by Martins Penna, *The Best Mayor, the King (El mejor alcalde, el Rey)* by Lope de Vega, *Tartuffe* by Molière, *The Inspector General* by Gogol.

The "nationalization" was realized keeping in mind the social objectives of the moment. Thus, for example, *The Best Mayor* . . . suffered profound alterations in the text of the third act, to such an extent that the authorship was attributable more to the adaptors than to the author. Lope wrote it when the historical moment demanded the unification of nations under the dominance of a king. The work exalts the just individual, the charitable, good, immaculate ruler who holds all power in his hands. It exalts charisma. Though this story was appropriate for Lope's time, for ours, in Brazil, it ran the risk of turning reactionary. For this reason the modification of the whole structure of the text was necessary in order to restore, centuries later, its original idea. On the other hand, *Tartuffe* was staged without the alteration of a single Alexandrian verse. At the time of its production, religious hypocrisy was being practiced widely by our own Tartuffes, who in the name of God, Country, Family, Morality, Freedom, etc., marched along the streets demanding punishments both divine and military for the impious. *Tartuffe* penetratingly reveals this mechanism that consists in transforming God into an active partner instead of maintaining Him in the appropriate position of Supreme Judge. There was no need to emphasize or cut any part of the original text, not even considering that Molière himself, in order to avoid "Tartuffian" censorship, felt obliged at the end of the play to pay tribute to the government. There it was sufficient to follow the text in all its simplicity to make the audience laugh: the work was nationalized.

This stage from the start offered some complications; for example, the style. Many people thought that the production of classic works was a return to the TBC and did not realize the greater scope of the new project. When we staged Molière, Lope, or Machiavelli, it was never our intention to recreate the conventional style of each one of these authors. In order to be able to insert them into our time, these texts were treated as if they had no theatrical or national tradition behind them. Doing Lope we were not thinking of Alejandro Ulloa, nor were we thinking of the French casts when doing Molière. Our thoughts, rather, were on those to whom we wished to address ourselves, and on the human and social interrelations of the characters, valid both in other times and in our own. Of course we always arrived at a "style" but never in an *a priori* manner. For us this meant assuming the responsibilities that go with artistic creation, and it freed us from the limitations of copying.

Those who preferred the already familiar endorsed by the critics of the great cultural centers, were repelled: many reacted in this way. The great majority, however, felt fascinated by the adventure of understanding that a classic is universal only insofar as it is Brazilian. The "universal classic," that only Old Vic or the Comédie can do, does not exist. We too are the "universe." With regard to the interpretation, we dislocated another emphasis. The social interpretation came to the forefront. Instead of taking some debatable essences as the basis of their interpretation, the actors began to build their characters from their relationships with the others. That is, the characters started to be created from the outside inward. We realized that the character emanates from the actor, and is not a figure who floats afar until reached in a moment of inspiration. But from which actor does he emanate? Each human being creates his own character in real life. He has a particular way of laughing, walking, speaking, with habits of language, thought, and feeling: the rigidity of each human being is the character that each one creates for himself. However, each one is capable of seeing, hearing, feeling, thinking, and being moved more than in everyday life. The actor, once he is freed of his daily conditioning — extending the limits of his perception and expression — restricts his possibilities to those required by the interrelations in which his character is involved.

Once this stage was developed it was easy to verify that if the preceding one had concentrated excessively on the exhaustive analysis of singularities, this one had been reduced too much to the synthesis of universalities. One presented nonconceptualized existence; the other, abstract concepts. It was necessary to attempt to synthesize the two.

Fourth Stage: Musicals

The Arena produced a vast number of musical shows. Every Monday it presented performances of musicians and singers, bringing the shows together under the general title of "Bossa-Arena," with production by Moracy do Val and Solano Ribeiro. The series included even some experimental works of Paulo José, such as *Little Story* and *The Children's Crusade*. The shows ranged from the one produced in cooperation with the "Opinion" group of Rio de Janeiro — the musical *Opinion*, in which Nara Leão, Maria Bethania, Zé Keti, and João do Vale participated — to the one-man show: *The Creation of the World According to Ari Toledo*, as well as *An American in Brasília* by Nelson Lins de Barros, Francisco de Assis, and Carlos Lyra; *Arena tells Bahia*, with Gilberto Gil, Gal Costa, Tomré, Piti, and Caetano Veloso;

and *Wartime* with Maria Bethania. Others, of a more episodical and circumstantial nature, were also presented. All shows considered, the one that seems most important to me, at least in the sequence of this brief history, is *Arena tells about Zumbí*, by Guarnieri and Boal, with music by Edu Lobo.

Zumbí had many aims and succeeded in several. Its fundamental aim was the destruction of all the theatrical conventions that had become obstacles to esthetic development of the theater. Still more was desired: to tell a story not from the cosmic perspective, but from an earthly perspective clearly localized in time and space — the perspective of the Arena Theater and members of its company. The story was not narrated as if it existed autonomously; it existed solely in reference to the narrator.

Zumbí was a work that warned against all present and future evils. And given the newspaper-like nature of the text, it required connotations that were familiar to the audience. In works that demanded connotation the text was put together in such a way as to stimulate the spectators' response. This way of composing the text, together with its special nature, determines a simplification of the structure. Morally, the text is Manichaean, which belongs to the best tradition of the medieval religious theater, for instance. And in the same way, and for the same reasons that religious drama of the Middle Ages required all the theatrical means available, also in the case of *Zumbí*, the text had to be supported by music, which in this work was designed to prepare the audience to receive the ideas presented through song.

Zumbí destroyed conventions, all the ones it could. It even destroyed what must be recovered. It destroyed empathy. Not being able to identify itself at any time with any character, the audience often took the position of a cold spectator of consummated events. And empathy must be reconquered — but within a new system that will incorporate it and make it perform a compatible function.

Need for the "Joker"

The production of *Arena tells about Zumbi* was perhaps the greatest success — both artistically and in terms of its impact on the audience — achieved by the Arena Theater. Successful in relation to the audience because of its polemical nature, its attempt to revive discussion of an important episode in the nation's history — utilizing for this purpose a modern perspective — and for having revalidated the struggle of the Blacks as an example of another that we must wage in our own time. Artistically successful for having destroyed some of the most traditional and deeply rooted theatrical conventions, which persisted as mechanical, esthetic limitations on creative freedom.

With *Zumbi* the phase of the "destruction" of the theater — of all its values, rules, precepts, formulas, etc. — reached its culmination. We could not accept the existing conventions, but it was not yet possible for us to offer a new system of conventions.

The convention is a created habit: it is neither good nor bad in itself. We should not, for example, categorize as good or bad the conventions of the traditional naturalistic theater. They were and are useful in certain times and circumstances. The Arena Theater itself, in the period from 1956 to 1960, made ready use of realism, of its conventions, techniques, and procedures. That use answered the social and theatrical need of showing Brazilian life on stage, especially in its outward appearance. We were more interested in showing real things (borrowing terms from Brecht) than in revealing how things really are. For this we used photographic techniques. In the same way, we were ready to utilize the tools of any other style, as long as they met the esthetic and social needs of our organization as an activist theater, that is, a theater that attempts to influence reality and not merely reflect it, even if correctly.

Reality was and is in transition; stylistic tools, on the other hand, are perfect and finished. We want to examine a reality in the process of modification, and we only had available for our use styles that were unmodifiable or unmodified. These structures clamored for their own destruction, in order that, in theater, the process could be captured. And we wanted to capture it almost daily — newspaper theater.

Zumbí, first of the series *Arena tells* . . . disorganized the theater. For us, its main mission was to create the chaos that was necessary as a preliminary step for the initiation, with *Tiradentes*, of the stage proposing the new system. This healthy disorder was brought about mainly through four techniques.

The first consisted in an actor-character separation. To be sure, this was not the first time that actors and characters had been separated. More precisely: so it was when theater was born. In Greek tragedy, first two, then three, actors took turns in the interpretation of all the fixed characters of the text. For this they used masks, which prevented the confusion of the public. In our case, we also tried the use of a mask — not a material mask but rather a set of mechanized actions and reactions of the character. Each one of us, in real life, exhibits a type of pre-established, mechanized behavior. We create habits of thought, of language, of profession. All our relations in daily life are patterned. These patterns are our "masks," as are also the "masks" of the characters. In *Zumbí*, we were trying to maintain the permanent mask of the character being interpreted, independently of the actors performing each role. Thus the characteristic violence of King Zumbí was maintained regardless of which actor might be performing it in each scene. The "asperity" of Don Ayres, the "youth" of Ganga Zona, the "sensuous" nature of Gongoba, etc., were not linked to the physical type or personal characteristics of any actor. It is true that the quotation marks themselves give an idea of the generical nature of each "mask." Certainly, this procedure would never serve for the performance of a play based on the works of Proust or Joyce. But *Zumbí* was a Manichaean text, a text of good and evil, of right and wrong — a text of exhortation and combat. And for this kind of theater that type of interpretation was perfectly adequate.

But one need not look back to Greek tragedy for examples of the separation of actor and character, for many can be found in modern theater. *He Who Says Yes* by Brecht and *Stories to be Told* by the Argentinian playwright Osvaldo Dragún are two examples. They resemble, and at the same time differ from, *Zumbí*. In the Argentinian play, at no time is a dramatic conflict established; the text tends toward lyrical narration: the characters are narrated as in poetry and the actors behave as if they were dramatizing a poem. Also in the Brecht text, what has happened in the past with a military patrol is narrated from a distance — the death of a comrade is shown before the judges: "present time" is the narration of the event that has happened, not the event that is happening.

Now in *Zumbí* — and this is neither a virtue nor a defect — each moment of the play was interpreted "presently" and "conflictually," even though the "montage" of the performance might not allow one to forget the presence of the story's group-narrator; some actors remained in the time and place of the spectators, while others traveled to other places and times. The result of this was a kind of "patchwork quilt" formed of small fragments of many plays, documents, and songs.

Examples of separation are innumerable. Let us remember the "Frères Jacques" and the whole "Living Newspaper" movement in the American theater. One of the plays of this movement, "$E=MC_2$," told the story of atomic theory since Democritus, and of the atomic bomb since Hiroshima, advocating the peaceful utilization of this type of energy. The scenes were totally independent of each other and were related only because they referred to the same theme.

In general, the desire to place each of our works in the context of the history of theater is in vogue; and often one forgets to insert it in the context of Brazilian society. Thus even though the history of theater is full of precedents, the important aspect in this new procedure of the Arena had to do mainly with the need to eliminate the influence that the previous realist phase had had on the case, during which each actor tried to exhaust the psychological nuances of each character, and to which he devoted himself exclusively. In *Zumbí* each actor was forced to interpret the totality of the play and not merely one of the participants in the conflicts portrayed.

By obliging all the actors to interpret all the characters, the second technical objective of this first experiment was achieved. All the actors were grouped into a single category of narrators; the spectacle ceased to be realized from the point of view of each character and came to be narrated by a team, according to collective criteria: "We are the Arena Theater" and "We, all together, are going to tell a story, what we all think about the subject." We were thus able to reach a level of "collective" interpretation.

The third technique used with success to create chaos was stylistic eclecticism. Within the same performance we ranged from the simplest and most "soap opera"-type melodrama to the style of circus and vaudeville. Many thought that the chosen path was dangerous and the Arena received several warnings regarding its limits; a real attempt was made to draw a decisive line between the "dignity of art" and the "provocation of laughter, no matter what." Curiously though, the warnings were always aimed at the comic elements, never at the melodrama, which, at the opposite extreme, ran the same risks. Perhaps this was due to the fact that our public and our critics had gotten used to the melodrama, and the opportunities to laugh are very scarce in our times and in our country.

Also in relation to style, and not only to the genre, a healthy esthetic chaos was introduced. Some scenes, such as that of "Banzo," tended to be expressionistic, while others, such as the one of the priest and Lady Dueña, were realistic; the Ave Maria was symbolist and the one of "the twist" bordered on surrealism, etc.

In theater any break stimulates. The traditional rules of playwriting recommend comic relief as a form of stimulus. Here a sort of "stylistic relief" was achieved and the public welcomed the brusque, violent changes.

One further technique was used. Music has the power independently of the concepts, to prepare the audience in an immediate way, imaginatively, for the reception of simplified texts which can only be absorbed through the experience reason-music. Let me clarify with an example: without music no one would believe that on the "placid banks of Ypiranga a heroic and thunderous cry was heard" (Brazilian National Anthem) or that "like a white swan on moonlit nights, something glides on a blue sea" (Hymn of the Brazilian Navy). In the same manner and because of the simple way in which the idea is presented, nobody would believe "it is a time of war" if it were not for the music of Edu Lobo.

Finally, using these four techniques, *Zumbí* had the main esthetic mission of synthesizing all the preceding phases of the artistic development of the Arena Theater.

During the whole realist period, the Arena's dramaturgy as well as the acting sought above all, the detail. As the "Joker" says in *Tiradentes*, "works in which they ate spaghetti and made coffee and the audience learned just that: how to make coffee and eat spaghetti — things it already knew." It was a whole period in which the main concern was the search for particulars, aiming at the most minute and truthful description of Brazilian life in all its external, visible aspects. The exact reproduction of a life as it is — this was the principal goal of that entire period. That path, although necessary in its moment, entailed a great risk of nullifying the work of art. Art is a form of knowledge: the artist, therefore, has the obligation of interpreting reality, making it understandable. But if instead of interpreting, he limits himself to reproducing it, he will be failing to comprehend it or to make it comprehensible. And the more reality and art tend to be identical, the more useless will be the latter. The criterion of similarity is the measure of inefficacy. The playwrights did not want to limit themselves merely to imitation, but the truth was that, nevertheless . . . the utilization of naturalist instruments reduced the possibilities of analysis. The texts were becoming ambiguous and ambivalent: who was the hero, the petty bourgeois Tião, or Octavio the proletarian? What was the solution of José da Silva — to leave everything as it was and die of starvation, or to fight as a guerrilla? (Characters in *They Don't Wear Tuxedos* and *Revolution in South America*). In the succeeding stage, when the "nationalization of the classics" was attempted, the aims were in contraposition: we began to deal simply with ideas vaguely embodied in fables — *Tartuffe, The Best Mayor*, etc. The reproduction of life in the time of Louis XIV or in the Middle Ages mattered little to us. Don Tello and Tartuffe were not human beings placed in their time, but wolves of La Fontaine that closely resembled Brazilians: Dorina and Pelayo were wolves in sheep's clothing. The whole cast of characters was made up of symbols that became significant because they reflected traits similar to those of our people.

It was necessary to synthesize: on one hand, the singular; on the other, the universal. We had to find the typical particular.

The problem was solved, in part, by utilizing an episode from the history of Brazil, the myth of Zumbí, and attempting to fill it with data and recent events well known to the public. For example: the speech given by Don Ayres when he takes office was almost totally written on the basis of newspaper clippings of speeches contemporary with the play's production. (More specifically, the speech delivered by the dictator Castelo Branco at the Command Post of the Third Army, regarding the police role that soldiers should perform "against the internal enemy.")

Actually, the true synthesis had not been achieved; we had barely managed — and it was no small accomplishment — to juxtapose the "universal" and the "singular" by amalgamating them: on one hand, the mythical story with all the structure of the fable, intact; on the other hand, journalism effected by making use of the most recent events of national life. The union of the two levels was almost simultaneous, resulting in an approximation of the text to the typical particular.

Zumbí performed its function and represented the end of one stage of research. The stage of "destruction" of the theater was concluded, and the beginning of new forms was proposed.

"Joker" is the system proposed as a permanent form of theater — dramaturgy and staging. It brings together all the experiments and discoveries previously made in the Arena Theater; it is the sum of all that happened before. And in bringing them together, it also coordinates them. In this sense, it is the most important leap forward in the development of our theater.

Goals of the "Joker"

The proposal of a new system does not arise out of a vacuum. It always appears in answer to esthetic and social stimuli and needs. Exhaustive studies have shown the structure of Elizabethan texts to be a consequence of the social conditions of their time, of their public, and even of the special characteristics of their theater as a building. Shakespearean plays generally start with scenes of violence — servants fighting *(Romeo and Juliet)*, a mass protest movement *(Coriolanus)* — or with the appearance of a ghost *(Hamlet)*, of three witches *(Macbeth)*, of a monster *(Richard III)*, etc. It was not by chance that the playwright chose to start his plays in such a manner. A great deal has been written about the rowdy behavior of his public, including some rather curious practices. For example, the romantic language of the oranges: a gentleman wishing to court a lady in the audience would buy a dozen oranges, shouting to the vendor, unmindful of the fact that at that moment a tender scene might be in progress on stage. Afterward the same vendor would see that the oranges reached the lady in question. The response was implicit in the lady's behavior. If she returned the package, it was better not to insist; if she returned only half, who knows? If she kept them, then hopes were high. And if, thank goodness, she ate them right there, during the "To be or not to be," there was no doubt — the couple would not be present at the end of the tragedy, preferring to create their own bucolic comedy at another place.

Obviously those would not be the best conditions for the development of the Maeterlinckian drama. Laurence Olivier, in his film *Henry V*, gives a precise image of the Elizabethan audience: shouts, insults, fights, direct threats to the actors, spectators circulating constantly everywhere, noblemen on the stage, etc. To quiet that audience, a decisive, vigorous introduction was needed. The actors had to make more noise than the audience. The methodology of Shakespearean playwriting thus came to conform to those conditions.

Also, technical advances influence the appearance of new styles: without electricity expressionism would be impossible. But there are other factors as well that act as determinants of theatrical form. The Volksbuhne, birthplace of the modern epic theater, would have been impossible without its sixty thousand proletarian members, just as the sexual aberrations, castrations and anthropophagy of Tennessee Williams would be impossible without the New York public. It would be absurd to offer Brecht's *Mother Courage* on Broadway or *Night of the Iguana* in the union halls of Berlin. Each public demands plays that assume its vision of the world.

In the underdeveloped countries, however, the custom was to choose the theater of the "great cultural centers" as a model and goal. The public at hand is rejected in favor of a distant public, of which one dreams. The artist does not allow himself to be influenced by those around him and dreams of the so-called "educated" or "cultured" spectators. He tries to absorb alien traditions without having a firm foundation in his native tradition; he receives a culture as if it were the divine word, without saying a single word of his own.

The "Joker" system was not a capricious creation; it was determined by the present-day characteristics of our society and, more specifically, of our Brazilian public. Its objectives are of an esthetic and economic nature.

The first problem to be solved consists in the presentation within the same performance, both of the play and its analysis. Obviously, the staging of any play already includes its own analytical criteria. For example, no two performances of *Don Juan* are alike, even though they are based on the same text of Molière. *Coriolanus* can be staged as a play of support or repudiation of fascism. The hero of *Julius Caesar* can be Marcus Antonius or

Brutus. The modern director can choose between the arguments of Antigone or Creon, or he can condemn both. The tragedy of Oedipus can be fate or his pride.

The need to analyze the text and to reveal this analysis to the audience; to focus the action according to a single, predetermined perspective; to show the point of view of the author or director — this need has always existed and has been met in diverse ways. The monologue generally offers the audience a particular angle from which it may view and understand the totality of the conflicts in the play. In Greek tragedy the chorus, which so often acts as a moderator, also analyzes the behavior of the protagonists. The "raisonneur" of Ibsen's plays rarely has a specifically dramatic function, showing himself throughout to be the author's spokesman. Frequently used also is the "narrator," such as the one created by Arthur Miller in *View from the Bridge* and, in a more limited way, in *After the Fall*. The protagonist addresses himself in an explanatory manner to someone who could be God as well as the psychoanalyst — it matters little to Miller and even less to us.

Those are some of the possible solutions, already developed. In the "Joker" system the same problem is present and a similar solution is offered. In all the techniques mentioned above, what is most objectionable to us is the camouflage with which the true intention is hidden. The functioning of the technique is concealed with embarrassment. We prefer the impudence of showing what it is and for what it is used. The camouflage ends up creating a "type" of character much closer to the other characters than to the spectator: choruses, narrators, etc. are inhabitants of fables and not of the society in which the spectators live. We propose a "Joker" who is a contemporary and neighbor of the spectator. For this it is necessary to restrict his "explanations"; it is necessary to move him away from the other characters, to bring him close to the spectators.

Within this system, the "explanations" given periodically are designed to make the performance develop on two different and complementary levels: that of the fable (which can use all the conventional imaginative resources of the theater), and that of the "lecture," in which the "Joker" becomes an exegete.

The second esthetic objective concerns the style. It is true that many successful plays use more than one style, as in the case of Ferenc Molnar's *Liliom* or Elmer Rice's *The Adding Machine* (realisms and expressionism for the scenes on Earth and in Heaven). But it is also true that the authors take great pains to justify the stylistic changes. Expressionism is acceptable provided the scene is in Heaven, but this is nothing more than a disguise for the realism which remains. Even in the movies, the famous *The Cabinet of Doctor Caligari* is nothing more than a realist film in disguise; in it apologies are made for the stylistic devices used, justifying them by the fact that the work deals with a vision of the world from a madman's point of view.

Zumbí itself, with all the liberties that it took, was unified by a general atmosphere of fantasy; all the scenes were in fact worked with the same instruments of fantasy. While stylistic variety was produced by differences in the manner of utilizing the instruments, unity resulted from working always with the same instruments. The body of the actor absorbed the functions of the ethical scenography of black and white, good and bad, love and hate, the tone at times nostalgic, other times exhortative, etc.

With the "Joker" we propose a permanent system of theater (structure of text and cast) which will contain all the instruments of all styles or genres. Each scene must be conceived, esthetically, according to the problems it presents.

Every unity of style entails an inevitable impoverishment of the procedures that can be utilized. Usually instruments of a single style are selected, the one that appears to be ideal for the main scenes of the play; then the same instruments are utilized in dealing with all the other scenes, even though they prove to be inadequate. Therefore, we decided to resolve the problems of each independently. Thus realism, surrealism, the pastoral, the tragicomedy, and any other genre or style are available to the director or author, without his being obliged for this reason to utilize them during the whole of the work or performance.

Of course, with this approach one runs a rather considerable risk of falling into total anarchy. In order to avoid this danger greater emphasis is placed on the "explanations," so that the style in which they are elaborated may become the general style of the play to which all the others must be referred. We are speaking here of writing plays that are fundamentally judgements, trials. And, as in a courtroom, the fragments of each intervention, or testimony, can have their own form, without damage to the particular form of the trial. In the "Joker" also: each chapter or episode can be treated in the manner that fits it best, without damage to the unity of the whole, which will be provided not by the limiting permanence of a form, but by the stylistic variety existing in reference to a single perspective.

It should be noted that the possibility of great variation in form is offered by the simple presence within the system of two completely opposite functions: the protagonic function, which is the most concrete reality, and the "Joker" function, which is the universalizing abstraction of the other. In them all styles are included and are possible.

The modern theater has emphasized originality too much. The two wars, the permanent war for liberation of the colonies, the rise of the oppressed classes, the advancement of technology, all act as a challenge for artists, who respond with a series of basically formal innovations. A rapidly evolving world determines also the enormous rapidity with which the theater evolves. But there is one difference which becomes an obstacle: each new scientific conquest lays the foundation for the next conquest, losing nothing and gaining all. On the other hand, each new conquest in the theater has meant the loss of all the previous gains.

Thus the principal theme of modern theatrical technique has come to be the coordination of all its conquests, in such a way that each new creation may enrich its heritage and not destroy it (replace it). And this must be done within a structure that is absolutely flexible, so that it can absorb the new discoveries and remain at the same time unchanged and identical to itself.

The creation of new rules and conventions in theater, within a structure remaining unaltered, allows the spectators to know at every performance, the possibilities of the game. Soccer has pre-established rules, rigid structure of penalties and off-sides, which does not hinder the improvisation and surprise of each play. The game would lose all interest if each match were played in accordance to rules made up for that match alone, if the fans had to learn during the match the rules governing it. Previous knowledge is indispensable to full enjoyment.

In the "Joker" the same structure will be used for *Tiradentes* and *Romeo and Juliet*. But within this unchanging structure, nothing will impede the originality of each scene or chapter, episode or explanation.

Not only in sports can we find comparable examples: the spectator sees a painting and, upon examining a part, he can locate it in the totality that is also visible. The detail of a mural is seen simultaneously isolated and inserted in the whole. Theater will only be able to achieve this effect if the public knows beforehand the rules of the game.

Finally, one of the esthetic objectives of the system — no less important than the rest — consists in trying to resolve the option between character-object and character-subject which schematically derives from the belief that thought determines action or, on the contrary, that action determines thought. The first position is exhaustively defended by Hegel in his poetics, and long before that, by Aristotle.

Both state, in quite similar terms, that dramatic action results from the free movement of the character's spirit. Hegel goes even further and, as if he were thinking with premonition of present-day Brazil, he asserts that modern society is becoming incompatible with theater, since all the characters of today are prisoners of a tangle of laws, customs, and traditions which increases as society becomes civilized and developed. Thus it happens that the perfect dramatic hero is the medieval prince — that is, a man who possesses all powers: legislative, executive and judicial — no doubt one of the dearest aspirations of some present-day politicians, medieval men at heart. Only by having absolute power in his hands will the character be able to "freely express the movements of his spirit"; if those movements compel him to kill, possess, attack, forgive, etc., nothing foreign to him could prevent him from doing it: concrete actions originate in the subjectivity of the character.

Brecht — the theoretician and not necessarily the playwright — defends the opposite position. For him, the character is a reflection of the dramatic action, action which develops by means of objective and objective-subjective contradictions; that is, one of the poles is always the economic infrastructure of the society, even though the other may be a moral value.

In the "Joker" the structure of conflicts is always infrastructural, though the characters may not be conscious of this underlying development, that is, though they may be free in the Hegelian sense.

Thus the intent is to restore the full freedom of the

character-subject within the strict outlines of social analysis. The coordination of that freedom prevents the subjectivist chaos characteristic of lyrical styles: expressionism, etc. It prevents the presentation of the world as a perplexity, as inexorable fate. And, we hope, it should prevent the mechanistic interpretations which reduce human experience to a mere illustration of compendiums. Many are the objectives of this system. Not all of them are esthetic nor did they originate in esthetics. Drastic limitation of the purchasing power of the public brought about a reduction in the consumption of superfluous products, the theater among them. Each situation must be faced squarely in its own sphere, not according to optimistic perspectives, and the facts are these: the theater lacks a consumers' market, it lacks human resources, it lacks official support for any campaign aimed at popularization, and official restrictions are overabundant (taxes and regulations).

Within this hostile panorama, with a staging obedient to the "Joker" system, it is possible to present any play with a fixed number of actors, independently of the number of characters. Each actor of each chorus multiplies his possibilities of interpretation. The reduction of the cost of staging makes the performance of all texts feasible.

Those are the objectives of the system. Achievement of them depends on the creation and development of two fundamental structures: the cast and the performance.

Structures of the "Joker"

In *Zumbí* all the actors interpreted all the characters. The distribution of roles was made in each scene without regard to the continuity; on the contrary, an effort was made to avoid it by not giving the same actor the same role twice. Disregarding the obvious differences, it was like a soccer team of ranch hands: all the players, no matter what their positions are, are always after the ball. In *Tiradentes* and within the "Joker" system, each actor has a pre-established position and moves according to the rules set up for that position. Not characters but functions are distributed to actors, in accordance with the general structure of the conflicts in the text.

The first function is the "protagonic" one, which in the system represents a concrete, photographic reality. This is the only function in which a perfect and permanent link between actors and character takes place: a single actor portrays a single protagonist. Here empathy occurs.

Several requirements must be met in carrying out this function, in which the actor should make use of Stanislavskian interpretation, in its most orthodox form. The actor cannot perform any task that exceeds the limits of the character as a human being: to eat he needs food, to drink he needs drink, to fight he needs a sword. He must behave like a character in *They Don't Wear Tuxedos*. The space in which he moves must be thought of in the terms of Antoine. A "protagonic" character must have the outlook of the character and not of the authors. His existence is never interrupted, although, simultaneously, the "Joker" may be analyzing some detail of the play: he will continue his action "really" like a character from another play, lost on a theater stage. He is the "slice of life," neorrealism, the *cinéma vérité*, the living documentary, the minutiae, the detail, the apparent truth, the real thing.

The actor must not only be guided by criteria of verisimilitude; his scenographic conception must do it too: his clothes, his other personal items must be as authentic as possible. Upon seeing him, the audience must always have the impression of the absent fourth wall, even though the other three may also be absent.

This function attempts to reconquer the empathy that is always lost every time a performance tends toward a high degree of abstraction. In these cases the audience loses immediate emotional contact with the character and its experience tends to be reduced to a purely rational knowledge. We need not concern ourselves — nor is this the time to do so — with the principal reasons for this fact; for now it is enough to recognize it. And it is a fact that empathy is achieved with greater ease when any character, in any play with any plot or theme, performs an easily recognizable task, of a domestic, professional, sportive, etc., nature.

Empathy is not an esthetic value: it is only one of the mechanisms of the dramatic ritual which can be put to good or bad use. In the Arena's realist stage of development its use was not always praiseworthy, and many times the recognition of true-to-life situations replaced the interpretative quality that theater must have. In the "Joker" this external empathy will be followed point by point by the exegesis. External recognition is attempted and allowed as long as the analysis of that externalization is presented simultaneously.

The protagonist does not coincide necessarily with the main character. In *Macbeth* it can be Macduff; in *Coriolanus* it can be one of the commoners; in *Romeo and Juliet* it could be Mercutius if it were not for his premature death; in *King Lear* it could be the jester. The character whom the author wishes to link empathically with the public performs the protagonic function.

If we could separate the *ethos* and the *dianoia* — and we can

only do it for didactic purposes — we would say that the protagonist assumes an ethical behavior and the "Joker" a
dianoethic one.
The second function of the system is the "Joker" himself.
We could define this function as the exact opposite of the
protagonist's.
The "Joker's" is a magical reality; he creates it. If necessary, he invents magic walls, combats, soldiers, armies. All the
other characters accept the magic reality created and described
by the "Joker." To fight, he uses an invented weapon; to ride, he
invents a horse; to kill himself, he believes in the dagger that does
not exist. The "Joker" is polyvalent; his function is the only one
that can perform any role in the play, being able even to replace
the protagonist when the latter's realistic nature prevents him
from doing something. Example: the second act of *Tiradentes*
starts with the protagonist riding in a scene of fantasy; and since it
would not be prudent to come on stage with a horse, this scene is
performed by the actor who functions as the "Joker," riding on a
wooden horse (thus saving on the oats). . . . Every time situations such as these occur, the coryphaeus (chorus leader) will
perform, momentarily, the function of the "Joker."
The outlook of the "Joker"-actor must be that of the author
or adaptor which is assumed to be above and beyond that of the
other characters in time and space. Thus in the case of
Tiradentes, he will not have the outlook and knowledge possible
for Brazilian dissidents of the eighteenth century; on the contrary, he will always have in mind the events that have taken
place since then. This is to be effected on the level of history and
on the level of the story itself since, in this aspect, he represents
also the author or recreator of the story, knowledgeable of begin-
nings, middles, and ends. He knows, therefore, the development
of the plot and the objective of the play. He is omniscient. But
when the "Joker"-actor performs not only that function in general but also takes the role of one of the characters, then he
acquires only the outlook of the character he is interpreting.
In this way, all the theatrical possibilities are conferred upon
the "Joker" function: he is magical, omniscient, polymorphous,
and ubiquitous. On stage he functions as a master of ceremonies,
raisonneur, kurogo, etc. He makes all the explanations, verified
in the structure of the performance, and when necessary, he can
be assisted by the coryphaeus or the choral orchestra.

The other actors are divided into two choruses: deuteragonist and antagonist, each one having its own coryphaeus. Actors of the first chorus can perform any role supportive of the protagonist, that is, roles that represent the latter's central idea. Thus, for example — in the case of *Hamlet* — Horatio, Marcellus, the players, the ghost, etc. This is the "good" chorus (chorus of the hero). The other, the bandit-chorus, the "bad" chorus, is made up of the actors who represent adversary roles. In the sample example: King Claudius, Queen Gertrude, Laertes, Polonius, etc.

The choruses do not have a fixed number of actors; they may vary from one episode to another. There will be two types of costumes: the basic one relating to the function and the chorus to which the function belongs; another related not to each character to which the function belongs; another related not to each character but to the different social roles that he will perform during the conflict of the play. Only one costume will be allowed for each social role: army, church, proletariat, aristocracy, judicial power, etc. It may happen that two or more actors performing the same role will be on stage at the same time — the role of soldier, for example. In this case the costume must be such that it can be used by a number of actors simultaneously, and that it allows the public to identify visually all the actors who perform the same role. Otherwise, there would have to be as many costumes as characters.

Actors and actresses without regard to sex, will be able to perform masculine or feminine roles, with the exception, of course, of the scenes in which sex determines the dramatic action. Actors of opposite sex will have to perform love scenes, for example, unless the Arena, unexpectedly, decides to perform Tennessee Williams. Something highly unlikely.

Completing the structure is the choral orchestra — guitar, flute, and percussion. The three musicians will also have to play other string, wind, and percussion instruments. Besides the musical support it provides, the orchestra must sing, alone or together with the coryphacus, all the comments of an informative or imaginative nature.

This is the basic structure of the system which will have to be flexible enough to adapt itself to the staging of any play. For example, in the event that the play needs the presence of three groups in conflict, the tritagonist chorus can be created while maintaining all the rest of the scheme intact. In a play like *Romeo and Juliet* the number of protagonists can be increased to two, having only one "Joker," or relegating his functions to the choral leaders, who for their part will act as the heads of the houses of Montague and Capulet. In plays where no special emphasis is placed on the protagonist, this function can be abolished and two "Jokers," who will absorb the choral leaders' functions, can be created. Finally, if one of the forces in conflict should need only one or two actors during the greater part of the development of the play, the choral leaders can be maintained while grouping all the other actors into a single, "Joker's" chorus.

The adaptation of each text in particular will determine the necessary modifications, keeping the structure of the cast. The "Joker" will also have a permanent "structure of performance" for all plays. This structure is divided in seven main parts: dedication, explanation, episode, scene, commentary, interview, and exhortation.

Every performance will begin always with a dedication to a person or event. It can be a song sung by all, a scene, or simply a recited text. It can also be a sequence of scenes, poems, texts, etc. In *Tiradentes*, for example, the dedication is composed of a song, a text, a scene, and a song sung in chorus, dedicating the performance to José Joaquim da Maia, the first man who took concrete measures for the liberation of Brazil.

The explanation consists in a break in continuity of the dramatic action. Always written in prose and recited by the "Joker" in the terms of a lecture, it attempts to place a focus on the action from the perspective of the one who presents it, in this case, the Arena Theater and its constituents. It can utilize any of the resources proper to a lecture: reading the texts, documents, letters, slides, items from the daily newspapers, films, maps, etc. It can go so far as to undo some of the scenes in order to emphasize or correct them, bringing in others — in the case of adaptations — that do not appear in the original text, to achieve greater clarity. For example, in staging the case of the indecisive Hamlet, a scene showing the decisive Richard III can be presented. The explanations mark the general style of the play: lecture, forum, debate, tribunal, exegesis, analysis, defense of a thesis, etc. The introductory explanation presents the cast, the author, the adaptor, as well as the techniques utilized, the need to renovate the theater, the objectives of the text, etc. All the explanations can and should be extremely dynamic, changing as the play is staged in other cities or on other dates. In this way, when the play is presented in a town where theater has never before been performed, it will be more appropriate to explain theater in general than the "Joker" in particular. If on the day of the performance some important event occurs which is related to the theme of the play, that relationship should be analyzed. We want to emphasize strongly the transitory and ephemeral nature of this permanent system: objectively, its intent is to increase the flexibility in order to assure reflection of the performance in its moment, day, and hour, without being reduced to the hour, the day, or the moment.

The general structure will be divided into episodes, which will group together more or less interdependent scenes. The first sequence will always have one episode more than the second: 2 and 1, 3 and 2, 4 and 3, etc.

A scene or incident is of small magnitude, but complete in itself, and contains at least one variation in the qualitative development of the dramatic action. It can be in dialogue form, song form, or limited to the reading of a speech, a poem, a news item, or document that determines a qualitative change in the system of conflicting forces.

The scenes are interconnected by the comments written preferably in rhymed verses, sung by the coriphaei or the orchestra, or by both, and which have the purpose of connecting one scene to another in a fantastic manner. Taking into consideration that each scene has its own style, whenever it proves necessary, the commentaries shall advise the audience with respect to each change.

The interviews do not have a specific structural placement of their own since their appearance always depends on the expository needs. Many times the playwright feels obliged to reveal to the audience the true state of mind of a character, but nevertheless he cannot do it in the presence of the other characters. For example, Hamlet's actions can only be understood if his wish to die is exposed, but this cannot be done in front of the king and queen, not even in front of Horatio or Ophelia. Shakespeare makes use of the monologue, then, as a more practical, more rapid expedient of direct communication. It can also happen that that informative need will be present throughout all the action. O'Neil solved the problem by having his characters in *Strange Interlude* say the "spoken" text and the "thought" text in different tones, aided by the lighting and other theatrical resources. In *Days Without End* the presence of two actors for the role of John Loving proved to be necessary: one interpreted John, the visible part of his personality, and the other interpreted Loving, his inner life. Also the aside has long been used in the history of theater. The fact that this technique is out of fashion today is perhaps due to the fact that the aside creates a parallel structure of intermittent nature which confuses the action instead of explaining it.

In the "Joker" this need is met with the utilization of resources that belong to other, extra-theatrical rituals, during sporting events (soccer, boxing, etc.) in the intervals between one period (quarter, round, inning) and another, or during the momentary suspensions of play, when commentators interview the athletes and experts, who inform the public directly about what has happened on the field.

In this manner, every time it is necessary to show the "inside" of the character, the "Joker" will stop the action momentarily so that the character may explain his reasons. When this occurs, the interviewed character is to maintain his consciousness as a character, that is, the actor refrains from assuming his own consciousness of "here and now." In *Tiradentes* the whole political incident regarding the Viscount of Barbacena and the collection of royal taxes would inevitably be attributed to his "kind heart" and not to the coldness of his thinking if his thoughts were confided to the spectators through asides or similar techniques — which does not happen when his thoughts are revealed through an interview. The spectators should be allowed to ask their own questions, as in a live program before an audience. The interviews are open.

Finally, the last part of the performance's structure consists of the exhortation, in which the "Joker" incites the audience in accordance with the theme dealt with in each play. It can be done in the form of recited prose or choral song, or in a combination of both.

Those are the basic structures of the system. We repeat a statement made previously: the system is permanent only within the transitoriness of theatrical techniques. It does not pretend to provide definitive solutions for esthetic problems. What it does pretend to do is to make theater possible again in our country. And with it goes the intention to go on thinking that theater is worthwhile.

Nowadays heroes are not well thought of. All the new theatrical trends speak ill of them, from the neoromantic neorealism of recent American Dramaturgy which delights in dissecting failure and success to the new Brechtianism without Brecht.

In the American case the propagandistic ideological objective of the exposure of failure is obvious: it is always good to show that there are people in worse situations than ours — this reassures the more sensible audience, whose members easily give thanks for the financial ability that made it possible for them to buy theater tickets, or who feel thankful for their little domestic happiness, in contrast with the characters tormented by vices, schizophrenia, neurosis and other illnesses of the daily psychoanalysis. The hero, whoever he may be, always carries within himself a willful movement, and the "no"! The American theater, on the contrary, must always say "yes" in its commercial submissiveness. Its main function is to tranquilize and sedate.

In the case of "neo-Brechtianism," the problem becomes complicated. One should ask, was it Brecht who eliminated the heroes, or was it the interpretations made by some of the more avid students of his work? Perhaps a look at some specific examples will be of help.

In one of his poems, Brecht tells stories about heroes, among them the story of Saint Martin the Charitable. He relates that one cold night during a rigorous winter, while walking along the street, the saint found a poor man dying of cold and "heroically" did not hesitate: he tore his cape in two and gave half of it to the poor man. Both died frozen, together! We ask: Was Saint Martin a hero, or, let us say it with moderation out of consideration for his sainthood, did he commit a thoughtless act? . . . There is no criterion of heroism that recommends stupidity. The heroism of Saint Martin is not demythicized for one simple reason: it is not heroism.

In another poem, also about heroes, Brecht emphasizes the fact that when a general wins a battle, thousands of soldiers fight side by side with him; when Julius Caesar crosses the Rubicon, he takes a cook with him. Obviously Brecht does not criticize the hero for not knowing how to cook nor the general for fighting accompanied by the soldiers. Brecht increases the number of heroes without destroying any of them.

Still, we find the assertion that Brecht debunks heroes. The example of Galileo before the tribunal of the Inquisition is cited, with Galileo "cowardly" denying the earth's motion. The critics say that if Galileo were a hero he would continue to affirm heroically that the earth moves and would endure the fire even more heroically. I prefer to think that in order to be a hero, it is not absolutely necessary to be dumb — and I even dare to imagine that a certain dose of intelligence is a basic requirement. To attribute heroism to an act of stupidity is a mystification. The heroism of Galileo was to lie, because to tell the truth would have been stupidity.

Brecht does not lash out at heroism per se, which in fact is nonexistent, but rather he censures certain concepts of heroism. And each social class has its own. In one of his poems Brecht writes that man must know how to tell the truth and to lie, to hide and to expose himself, to kill and to die. This sounds very different from the Kipling hero of "If" (". . . you will be a man, my son"). On the other hand, Brecht's words approach the teachings of Maoism regarding guerrilla tactics: One should only attack the enemy face to face when one is proportionally ten times stronger than he. Listening to Mao, Orlando would become even more *furioso* than when he listened to his uncle; the heroism of the Amadises and the Cids was determined by serfdom and sovereignty and anyone who attempts to re-edit it out of those structures will necessarily have to fight against windmills and wineskins before the curious eyes of prostitutes who were Castilian ladies in other times. Such was the fate of Don Quixote and such it will always be. The heroes of one class will always be the Quixotes of the class that follows it. The enemy of the people, Dr. Stockman, is a bourgeois hero. What does his heroism consist of? If worse comes to worst, he is capable of choosing to bring about the ruin of his town, for he only considers honorable the stance of denouncing the pollution of the thermal waters, the only or principal source of income for the municipality. In Ibsen's text, the contradiction between the need for bourgeois development of the city and the moral values preached by its citizens, is exposed. Stockman keeps his values and commits the error of "purity" — therein lies his special type of heroism. We could condemn him because we know that the real solution (provided we take into account the truth of a class other than the bourgeoisie) is not the one proposed by Stockman and is not even contained in the terms of the problem presented in the play. But if we condemn him, we will condemn not only his heroism, but also the bourgeoisie and all its values, including the moral ones. The heroism of Stockman is determined and endorsed by the bourgeois value structures that support and shape him. Each class, caste, or estate has its own hero, who is nontransferable. Therefore, the hero of one class will only be understood with the criteria and values of that class. The oppressed classes will be able to "understand" the heroes of the dominant classes while the domination continues, including moral domination. The Cid, for example, heroically risked his life in defense of Alfonso IV and heroically endured humiliation as a reward. Today the Cid, very heroically, would take his lord to a Labor Court and organize pickets in front of the factory doors, in the face of tear gas bombs and police bullets. The Cid-vassal was not foolish for having done what he did, nor would the Cid-proletarian be foolish for doing what he would. He was and will be a hero.

In dealing with heroes, literature can as easily present them as actual human beings as it can mythicize them. The way they are used depends solely on the purposes of each work. Julius Caesar was a sick man: this can be shown in the character, as the character can also be mythicized as a man of splendid health, or the author could simply avoid allusions to the matter.

Myth is the simplification of man. To this we have no objection. But the *myth*icization of man does not necessarily have to be *myst*ifying, for against the latter tendency many objections can and should be made. Nothing bothers us in the myth of Spartacus, although we know that perhaps his courage was not so great. Nothing bothers us in Gaius Gracchus and his agrarian reform. But the myth of Tiradentes disturbs us. Why?

The mythicizing process consists in magnifying the essence of real events and the behavior of the mythicized man. The myth of Gaisus Gracchus is a lot more revolutionary than the man Gaius Gracchus must have been. But it is true that the man distributed land among the peasants and for this reason was murdered by the landlords. The difference between the man and the myth is only one of quantity, since the essence of the behavior and the facts is the same: the essential facts are magnified while the circumstantial ones are eliminated. For example: his cook, his wines, and his love affairs do not form part of the myth though they may well have been an integral part of the man. For the creation of the myth Gaius Gracchus, it is irrelevant to know if the Roman had mistresses, or to know his tastes in food and drink, as it is equally irrelevant for the myth Tiradentes to present his illegitimate daughter and his concubine, even though the two of them might have been very relevant for him, a fact we do not doubt for a moment.

If the mythicization of Tiradentes had consisted exclusively in the elimination of secondary facts, there would have been no problems. But the dominant classes have the habit of "adapting" the heroes of other classes. Mythicization in these cases consists in obscuring, as if it were only circumstantial, the essential fact — promoting, on the other hand, the circumstantial characteristics to the condition of essence. Thus it happened with Tiradentes. The major importance of his deeds lies in their revolutionary content. Episodically, he was also a stoic. Tiradentes was a revolutionary in his time, as he would be in others, including our own. He was seeking, albeit romantically, to bring about the fall of an oppressive regime, wanting to replace it with another one, more apt to promote the well-being of his people. This is what he hoped to do for our country, and would surely have translated his desires into action had other events not made prior claim on his life: his suffering on the gallows, the acceptance of guilt, and the candidness with which he kissed the crucifix, etc. Today, it is customary to think of Tiradentes as the hero of Brazilian independence, but it is forgotten that he was a revolutionary hero, transformer of his reality. The myth is mystified. It is not the myth that must be destroyed; it is the mystification. It is not the hero who must be belittled; it is his struggle that must be magnified.

Brecht sang: "Happy is the people who needs no heroes." I agree. But we are not a happy people: for this reason we need heroes. We need Tiradentes.

Notes for Chapter 5

[1]The initials "N.N." stand for "no name," referring to actors whose names were not publicly acknowledged; unknown actors.

Appendices

Appendix A

Techniques of the "Joker" System

In the same way that in our daily life we live rituals without perceiving them as such, it is also difficult to become aware of them in theater; thus it becomes necessary to utilize certain techniques which allow the spectator to "see" the rituals as such, to see the social needs and not the individual wishes, to see the character's alienation without establishing an emphatic relationship with him.

This is much easier to achieve in cinema, due to the fact that the camera chooses the focus of attention for the spectator and concentrates his observation on a determined point. Thus Antonioni is the master of reification. The character portrayed by Alain Delon in *The Eclipse* has an intense desire for power, for being the first, being successful; and this is reified in the moment his car is shown (we had always seen it before running at a reckless speed) hanging from a crane, after having fallen in the river, or when, after making love with Monica Vitti, he again hangs up the six or seven telephones that immediately start ringing again and return him to alienation in the stock market world.

In theater the movement of the actors has to do what is done with the camera in the cinema.

1) *Breaking up the ritual.* The ritual is broken up in such a way as to obscure its familiar form: the tortured man reacts at a great distance from the torturer; the lover, from his loved one;

two boxers fight at a distance, etc. It is a question of breaking down a phenomenon into its parts, dismantling the mechanism so that the parts of that mechanism can be seen independently.

2) *Breaking up time.* It consists in placing the reactions before the actions. Thus the fighter suffers the blows before he is hit, and the vassal kneels before the sovereign enters, etc. Thus one of the alienated characters performs his function within the ritual even though the other member of the relationship is absent. The servile employee goes on being servile even when he has no one to serve; the peremptory general goes on giving orders even though there is no one to order; etc. The technique consists almost in removing the figure that determines a ritual and keeping the ritualized figure performing his ritual.

3) *Multiplication of optical perspectives.* The same ritual is reproduced in different optical perspectives, in the same manner that a goal in soccer is shown by press photographers from different perspectives, which reveal the player in different positions. *Bolivar* portrays a torturer multiplied by three, with all three executing the same movement, and at the same time far away from the tortured man.

4) *Application to one scene of the ritual of another.* When one wishes to reveal the class-oriented nature of a certain church at a certain time, the priest-believer ritual is applied to a landlord-peasant relationship. The master-slave ritual is applied to the love ritual; that of capitalist-worker, to the captain-soldier; etc. It is a technique whose significance lies in its ability to reveal the true essence of relationships, eliminating all the deceptive exterior features.

5) *Repetition of the ritual.* The ritual is repeated two or three times in identical or modified manner, in such a way that the spectator becomes aware of the strings that move this ritual.

6) *Simultaneous rituals.* To one ritual another is added, simultaneously, to serve as a point of comparison or to add a meaning.

7) *Metamorphosis.* an actor's changing his portrayal from one character to another can be done in such a way that, through a slow transformation, the new character who appears in the actor maintains the characteristics of the previous one. A dog that becomes a soldier, etc. When this is not desired, the change is effected by means of the "cut."

Appendix B

Social Mask

(Behavior: voice, movement, gesture, interpretation. Scenography: props, clothing, personal objects, colors, actual physical masks, whether from folklore or not, but of clear and immediate content, easily recognizable.)

1) *To which class does the character belong?* This is the basis for characterization of the social mask, behavior and scenography. Bourgeois or worker? Landlord or peasant? Owner of the land he works? In which regime? Bureaucrat? Manager? In short: does he rent his labor-power, or exploit his capital (money or land)?

2) *What is his basic social role?* Linked to the relations of production? Foreman? Manager? Secretary? Senior typist or assistant typist? Policeman in a large city or policeman in a small town, following orders of the federal bureaucracy or the sheriff and owner of the town? Drugs dealer? Driver for a colonel or of a taxi? How much does he earn in comparison to others with whom he is in closest and most permanent contact?

3) *Family relations?* Father? Mother? Son or daughter? Nephew? Uncle or aunt? What is the character's relationship in the family structure in comparison with the position he occupies in the structure outside of the family, in the area of production? Is the father the one who earns the most money in the family or is it the mother, and the father is retired or unemployed? Is the daugh-

ter a worker for her parents, or is she the one who ran away, works in a night club and maintains the family as a benefactor? 4) *Sex?* As above, the structure of the sexual and family relations compared to the structure of the relations of production. 5) *The social complex family-neighborhood-work.* Neighbors, companions, members of the same ball team, of the same society for neighborhood improvement, of the same class in school, of the same profession, etc.

The Unmasking

This consists in establishing all the structures of possible human relations for each case, comparing one with another: relations of production, work, sex, family, recreation. The character must be unmasked in all the roles he performs, in the interdependence of each role, in the translation of a role in one structure to another role in another structure, etc.

It is important to understand that men, fundamentally equal, are related among themselves according to unequal structures (family, work, school, neighborhood, etc.), determined basically by the infrastructure of the relations of production. If the latter change, inexorably all the other relations will change. In a revolutionary process, the important thing is to show the changes of the infrastructure, as well as the need for changes in the superstructure which will make the process advance.

Examples:

Guard:

> *proletarian* because he earns a salary by renting his labor-power (wears worker's clothes);
>
> *bourgeois* because, in certain instances, he defends the interests of the bourgeoisie and thinks like it (uses a top hat or something that the spectators decide is symbolic of the bourgeoisie);
>
> *companion* of the other guards (wears the colors of same soccer team, for example);
>
> *repressor* in the exercise of his functions, repressing for the purpose of maintaining order (uses a club or a gun);
>
> *father* of his children (wears anything that in the exercise can be recognized as symbolic of a father . . .), etc.

Priest:
    cross — sacrifice of Christ
    Bible — persuasion
    whip — repression
    cowherd's pants — landlord
Father:
    bourgeois, *head* of the family;
    partner of the mother in the exploitation of the children;
    boss of the daughter, whom he wants or needs to sell at a
    good price or to prevent from sleeping with someone at the
    risk of becoming pregnant and thus having one more mouth
    to feed.

Stages of the process

I. *Deritualizing and Unmasking*

Break down each character into the elements of his *social mask; analyze* the rituals which that mask must necessarily develop in its daily relationships, in the various complexes of structures and relationships: production, family, neighborhood, friends, etc.

II. *Analysis and Discussion*

Study of all the new possibilities of combining and transforming social masks and rituals; possible or necessary changes of the superstructures caused by changes in the infrastructure. For example: take the declaration that the police maintain order and will continue to do so, and proceed to the understanding that what will change, indeed profoundly, is the order that must be maintained. In this example, the policeman must take off his bourgeois top hat and put on a worker's helmet (herein lies the reason why American policemen bear more resemblance to astronauts than to their fellow workers).

II. *Re-ritualization and Remasking*

After selection of the new elements, new rituals are likewise selected, and the new structures are compared with the previous ones.

Index

Compiled by Marion Potter